Publisher: JKL Communications, Washington, D.C.

This publication is designed to provide accurate and authoritative information in regard to the subject matter covered. It is sold with the understanding that the publisher is not engaged in rendering legal, accounting, or other professional service. If legal advice or other expert assistance is required, the services of a competent professional should be sought. FROM A DECLARATION OF PRINCIPLES JOINTLY ADOPTED BY A COMMITTEE OF THE AMERICAN BAR ASSOCIATION AND A COMMITTEE OF PUBLISHERS.

Copyright 1994 © Peter S. Latham; Patricia H. Latham

All rights reserved.

Printed in the United States of America

IBSN 1-883560-03-9

SUCCEEDING IN THE WORKPLACE

ATTENTION DEFICIT DISORDER AND LEARNING DISABILITIES IN THE WORKPLACE : A GUIDE FOR SUCCESS

Edited By
PETER S. LATHAM, J.D. *and*
PATRICIA H. LATHAM, J.D.

DEDICATION

For our son John H. Latham and our daughter Kerry P. Latham

You have taught us so much.

This dedication is with pride in you and love always.

✍ ✍ ✍

TABLE OF CONTENTS

CHAPTER	PAGE
ABOUT THE AUTHORS	9
FOREWORD	12
1. WHAT IS ATTENTION DEFICIT DISORDER?	13
A. NATURE	13
B. SYMPTOMS	14
C. CAUSES	18
D. TREATMENT	20
1. MEDICATION	20
2. OTHER TREATMENTS	21
E. SUMMARY	22
2. WHAT ARE LEARNING DISABILITIES?	23
A. TYPES	23
1. PRACTICAL	24
2. MEDICAL	27
3. LEGAL	29
4. CONCLUSION	30
B. CAUSES	31
C. SUMMARY	32
3. STRATEGIES & ACCOMMODATIONS	34
A. OVERVIEW	34
B. POTENTIAL PROBLEM SITUATIONS TO CONSIDER	35

Table of Contents

    C. POSITIVE TRAITS — 35

    D. THE POWER OF PERSONALITY — 36

    E. STRATEGIES AND ACCOMMODATIONS — 36

        1. SKILL ENHANCEMENT — 37

        2. REASONABLE ACCOMMODATIONS — 37

        3. COMPENSATORY STRATEGIES — 40

        4. GENERAL STRATEGIES — 50

    F. SUMMARY — 51

4. FINDING THE JOB — 53

    A. GETTING ORGANIZED — 53

        1. KEEPING RECORDS OF THE JOB SEARCH — 53

        2. TIME MANAGEMENT — 54

    B. THE RESUME — 54

        1. DEVELOPING A RESUME WORKSHEET — 55

        2. THE ANATOMY OF A RESUME — 57

        3. HELPFUL TIPS IN PREPARING A RESUME — 58

        4. ACHIEVEMENT WORDS FOR RESUMES — 58

    C. FINDING JOB LEADS — 59

        1. RESOURCES FOR THE "HIDDEN" JOB MARKET — 59

        2. RESOURCES FOR THE "VISIBLE" JOB MARKET — 61

    D. THE COVER LETTER — 63

    E. THE APPLICATION — 63

        1. THE APPLICATION FORM — 63

        2. TIPS FOR PREPARING APPLICATIONS — 64

TABLE OF CONTENTS

    F. TELEPHONING — 65

    G. SUMMARY — 66

5. GETTING THE JOB — 67

    A. INTRODUCTION — 67

    B. THE JOB INTERVIEW — 67

    C. EMPLOYMENT TESTS — 69

    D. THE JOB OFFER — 70

        1. QUESTIONS TO ASK — 70

        2. DECLINING THE JOB OFFER — 72

        3. ACCEPTING THE JOB OFFER — 72

        4. LEAVING THE CURRENT POSITION — 73

    E. DISCLOSURE OF A DISABILITY — 74

        1. TALKING ABOUT THE DISABILITY — 74

        2. WHETHER TO DISCUSS THE DISABILITY WITH EMPLOYERS — 74

        3. WHEN TO DISCUSS THE DISABILITY — 76

    F. SUMMARY — 77

6. ON THE JOB — 78

    A. INTRODUCTION — 78

    B. GETTING AHEAD — 78

        1. ADVANCEMENT ISSUES — 78

        2. BE AN EXCELLENT EMPLOYEE — 79

        3. UP THE LADDER — 81

    C. IF THERE'S TROUBLE — 83

        1. SOCIAL REQUIREMENTS OF JOBS — 85

Table of Contents

    2. Signs of Trouble — 85

    3. Outside Help — 89

    4. Talking with the Supervisor — 90

    5. Termination — 91

  D. Summary — 92

7. PERSONAL STORIES — 93

  A. Introduction — 93

  B. Experiences — 94

  C. Summary — 102

8. RELATED ISSUES — 103

  A. Introduction — 103

  B. Career Counseling — 103

  C. Testing — 104

  D. Continuing Education and Training — 106

  E. Personal Financial and Tax Planning — 107

    1. Personal and Financial Planning — 107

    2. Tax Planning — 109

  F. Summary — 110

9. LEGAL RIGHTS — 111

  A. Introduction — 111

  B. Basic Principles, The Constitution and Statutes — 111

    1. The Constitution — 111

    2. Federal Statutory Law — 113

TABLE OF CONTENTS

a. The IDEA	113
b. The Rehabilitation Act of 1973	113
c. The Americans with Disabilities Act	113
3. THE RIGHT TO BE FREE FROM DISCRIMINATION	114
a. Overview	114
b. Individual With a Disability	114
1. Impairments Covered	115
2. Substantially Limits	116
3. Major Life Activities	117
c. Otherwise Qualified	119
1. Reasonable Accommodations	119
2. Undue Hardship	122
d. Solely By Reason Of	123
e. The RA or the ADA applies	124
f. Individualized Inquiry	124
4. AFFIRMATIVE ACTION	125
C. SPECIFIC PROBLEMS	125
1. WHAT IS A JOB?	125
2. ESSENTIAL FEATURES	126
3. JOB ADVERTISING	127
4. HIRING AND TESTING	127
5. PRE-EMPLOYMENT INQUIRIES	130
6. DISPARATE TREATMENT AND IMPACT	132
D. ENFORCEMENT	132

TABLE OF CONTENTS

1. REHABILITATION ACT OF 1973	132
2. AMERICANS WITH DISABILITIES ACT	133
E. SUMMARY	133

10. RESOURCES   134

APPENDICES   140

Appendix A - Sample Resume - Chronological	141
Appendix B - Sample Resume - Functional	143
Appendix C - Sample Resume - Combination	145
Appendix D - Sample Cover Letter	147
Appendix E - Sample Interview Questions	149
Appendix F - Sample Thank You Letter	153

About The Authors

This text has been edited (and authored in part) by Peter S. Latham, and Patricia H. Latham. The authors and their contributions are as follows:

DALE S. BROWN is a leader of the self-help movement for people with learning disabilities. She is a Program Manager for the President's Committee on Employment of People with Disabilities. She is the author of STEPS TO INDEPENDENCE FOR PEOPLE WITH LEARNING DISABILITIES and of over 100 articles on learning disabilities, with an emphasis on employment. She has visited almost every state, giving speeches on learning disabilities and related conditions, founded the Association of Learning Disabled Adults and served as the first President of the National Network of Learning Disabled Adults.

Dale S. Brown has been honored through awards from the American Speech and Hearing Association, the National Institute on Dyslexia, and the Department of Labor for her work with people with disabilities. In May 1993, she received the Arthur S. Flemming Award as one of ten outstanding federal employees under the age of forty for her "substantive work on the Americans with Disabilities Act." In January 1994, she received the TOYA Award (Ten Outstanding Young Americans) by the International Jaycees, for her work as an advocate for people with learning disabilities.

ELECTRONIC INDUSTRIES FOUNDATION ("EIF") is a not-for-profit foundation of the Electronic Industries Association based in Washington, D.C. EIF was established in 1975 to advance the independence and productivity of people with disabilities. EIF has pioneered methods of linking qualified persons with disabilities to job opportunities through a national program called PROJECT WITH INDUSTRY. Project staff members have contributed to this text based upon the many years of experience EIF has had in assisting individuals with disabilities in the workplace.

PETER S. LATHAM, J.D. and PATRICIA HORAN LATHAM, J.D., editors of the text and authors of certain chapters, are partners in the Washington, D.C.

ABOUT THE AUTHORS

law firm of Latham & Latham and founders of the National Center for Law and Learning Disabilities (NCLLD).

Peter S. Latham is a graduate of Swarthmore College, B.A. and the University of Pennsylvania, J.D. He is a member of the D.C. Bar, an arbitrator for the American Arbitration Association, served as a Naval Officer in Vietnam (1968-1969), was awarded the Navy Achievement Medal (with combat "V"), has lectured at the University of Virginia, written textbooks and articles on legal topics and is the producer and director of THE ABC'S OF ADD videos.

Patricia Horan Latham is a graduate of Swarthmore College, B.A. and the University of Chicago Law School, J.D. She is a member of the D.C. Bar, and the Virginia Bar, admitted to practice before the United States Supreme Court, a lecturer at Catholic University Law School and an arbitrator for the New York Stock Exchange and the American Arbitration Association.

The Lathams are authors of ATTENTION DEFICIT DISORDER AND THE LAW, LEARNING DISABILITIES AND THE LAW, and co-authors of ADD AND THE COLLEGE STUDENT. They have founded a special educational institution, served on the boards of disability organizations and written and spoken widely on disability law issues. They have practiced law for over twenty-five years. Both are listed in WHO'S WHO IN AMERICAN LAW.

KATHLEEN NADEAU, PH.D., received her Ph.D. in clinical psychology from the University of Florida in 1970. She is in private practice in the Washington, D.C. area, specializing in services in in the areas of learning disabilities and attention deficit disorder, including support groups for adults with ADD. She has published widely in these fields and has co-authored the following: LEARNING TO SLOW DOWN AND PAY ATTENTION, SCHOOL STRATEGIES FOR ADD TEENS, and ADD AND THE COLLEGE STUDENT. Currently, she is editing a comprehensive text on ADD in adults which is expected to be published in 1994.

PATRICIA O. QUINN, M.D., is a developmental pediatrician who has practised in the Washington, D.C. area since 1972. She is a graduate of Georgetown University Medical School. She was formerly Director of Medicine at the Georgetown University Child Development Center. She continues there as

ABOUT THE AUTHORS

Clinical Assistant Professor of Pediatrics and Child Psychiatry. Dr. Quinn specializes in child development and psychopharmacology. In her private practice, she sees high-risk infants and young children and follows patients through their school years and into adulthood.

Dr. Quinn works extensively in the areas of attention deficit disorder, hyperactivity, and learning disabilities. She gives workshops and has published widely in these fields, including the books PUTTING ON THE BRAKES: YOUNG PEOPLE'S GUIDE TO UNDERSTANDING ATTENTION DEFICIT HYPERACTIVITY DISORDER (ADHD) and THE "PUTTING ON THE BRAKES" ACTIVITY BOOK FOR YOUNG PEOPLE YOUNG WITH ADHD and ADD AND THE COLLEGE STUDENT.

FOREWORD

Attention deficit disorder with or without hyperactivity (ADD) and specific learning disabilities (LD) are neurologically based disorders which interfere with socialization, learning and working. They begin in childhood and often persist in some form into adulthood. After onset, feelings of frustration and failure for the individual and his family may result. Males are more often affected than females, and for this reason the term "he" is used throughout and is intended to refer to both males and females. These disabilities are often related and share a major attribute in common. They are "invisible" disabilities in the sense that they are seldom identifiable on first meeting the individual.

Nowhere do these disabilities affect the individual more than in the workplace. where failure strikes at the very core of self-esteem, the individual's bread-winning ability. Millions of dollars are lost to the economy every year as individuals fail to obtain jobs or fail to succeed at them. This book has been designed to address the workplace difficulties experienced by individuals with these disabilities. Representing the views of an inter-disciplinary team of experts, it is divided into 5 segments. **First**, Chapters 1 and 2 discuss the disabilities themselves and how they present in adulthood. **Second**, Chapters 3-6 discuss in detail strategies and accommodations for individuals with these disabilities, the techniques of finding a job, getting a job, advancing in a job, and handling job-related set-backs. Specific guidance in the preparation of resumes and the conducting of interviews is provided. Sample resumes and letters are included in an Appendix. **Third**, Chapter 7 presents the personal stories of individuals who have succeeded in the workplace despite these disabilities. **Fourth**, Chapter 8 discusses the related issues of career counseling and financial and tax planning. **Fifth**, and finally, Chapters 9 and 10 discuss the legal rights and other resources available to individuals with these disabilities.

The approach is general and non-technical in nature. It should not be considered to be a substitute for professional advice concerning particular situations. The book may assist individuals with these disabilities, their families, employers, educators, psychologists, and other professionals. It may be useful in facilitating transition from secondary school or college to the workplace - in courses and workshops.

1.

WHAT IS ATTENTION DEFICIT DISORDER?

Patricia O. Quinn, M.D.

A. NATURE

Attention Deficit Disorder (with or without hyperactivity) is a specific disorder of both children and adults that consists of difficulty with attention, impulse control, decision making, and distractibility. Hyperactivity is often a symptom, but this may be "outgrown" by adolescence and appear after that time as a fidgety restlessness and/or inability to sit still for long periods. The disappearance of the overt symptom of hyperactivity and its replacement with motor restlessness has led some professionals to think, mistakenly, that the disorder was "outgrown".

We now know that this is not the case, and that 40% to 60% of individuals with ADD continue to demonstrate symptoms into adulthood. In some adults these symptoms may not be as bothersome, but they are still present affecting overall performance and achievement. Many adults claim that ADD symptoms are responsible for general dissatisfaction with life accomplishments.

Attention deficit disorder occurs in anywhere from 5% to 10% of the general population. It is more commonly seen in males, but females, too, can have ADD. Women with ADD may not have the hyperactivity component and may even be described as shy and withdrawn. Studies have also shown that females tend to have more language problems, have difficulty with attention, frequently daydream, or appear disorganized.

The degree to which each adult is affected varies considerably, but most feel that they are underachieving. ADD is a hidden disability which often impacts upon the individual's performance in school, the workplace, and life in general. Some adults have learned over the years to compensate for some of their symptoms, while others (due to impulsivity) commonly present with a life of multiple job changes, marital difficulties, and frequent moves.

There are many causes of ADD, but the most common is probably genetic. In fact, adults frequently consider the diagnosis in themselves only when their children have been diagnosed with the condition. These adults will report childhood experiences that are similar to those of their children, and records and/or report cards can usually be found to bear out this impression. ADD can be seen at any age but usually has onset before the age of 7 years. In 1985, Paul Wender grouped the symptoms seen in adults with a previous history of ADD in childhood together and referred to them as Attention Deficit Hyperactivity Disorder - Residual Type. Other studies which have followed children with ADD into adulthood, also found persistence of symptoms with less stability and satisfaction in such areas as employment and marriage. Only half of one group at follow up was found to be functioning in the "normal" range, indicating that indeed these symptoms persist and interfere well into adulthood.

B. SYMPTOMS

How do you know if you have ADD as an adult? Wender's Utah criteria for ADD-R consist of the following: the individual must have had a history in childhood of the disorder; the adult must have symptoms of both hyperactivity and attentional deficit; and in addition must have two of the following characteristics: poor organization, poor concentration to task persistence, impulsivity or emotional lability.

UTAH CRITERIA FOR THE DIAGNOSIS OF ADD-RT

Childhood history of Attention Deficit Disorder*

> Fidgety, restless, always on the go, talking excessively
>
> Attention deficit
>
> Behavior problem in school
>
> Impulsivity
>
> Overexcitability
>
> Temper outbursts

Presence of ADD in adulthood*

> Persistent motor hyperactivity
>
> Attention deficits
>
> Affective lability
>
> Inability to complete tasks
>
> Hot temper, explosive short-lived outbursts
>
> Impulsivity
>
> Stress intolerance

*Must have the first two characteristics and two of the remaining characteristics.

Not all adults with ADD have all of these characteristics, but let's look at some of the practical ways that symptoms affect day-to-day experiences. Because of the symptoms described above, adults with ADD definitely have difficulty with **time management**. This manifests not only in estimating how long a task will take but also completing tasks on time. The complexity of getting everything done sometimes overwhelms adults with ADD, and so they do nothing - which leads to a tendency to procrastinate. This procrastination seems to be a hallmark of adults with ADD. Now, everyone procrastinates sometimes, but ADD individuals are often extreme and repeated procrastinators. The adult with ADD may take on too many tasks and projects that cannot be completed within a realistic period of time or with a realistic level of effort. As a result, many ADD adults display a tendency to give up on long-term projects. Additionally, they may have difficulty with activities of low interest such as managing paperwork or balancing checkbooks. Adults with ADD need to be strongly motivated to attack a task which is boring or routine. Many adults with ADD get into the position of letting the pressure of being "under the gun" of a deadline motivate them to improve task completion.

Distractibility is the inability to focus on just one thing. Competing stimuli vie for attention. This may lead to uncompleted tasks as the person goes from one project to another as it presents itself as more attractive or interesting. The person with ADD can get caught up in the present project leaving other projects and ideas incomplete. Chronic forgetfulness or lost belongings are seen as a result of distractibility and disorganization. Poor organizational skills can also lead to a tendency to begin tasks without waiting for directions or planning a strategy for completion. Prioritizing tasks can be difficult.

Impulsivity leads to quick decision making without thoughtfulness or long-range planning. This can lead to frequent job changes or leaving or starting a job on impulse. Impulsivity impairs the adult's ability to make decisions or to stick to a course of action. This may lead to problems following rules, delaying gratification or working for larger rewards. It may be difficult to inhibit behaviors as the situation demands, or to keep from changing plans. At times, individuals with ADD tend to just give up and quit.

There is likewise difficulty in **maintaining long-term relationships**. Individuals with ADD show less stability in their personal lives with more frequent changes of important intimate relationships. Impulsivity in speaking may lead the person with ADD to speak without considering what reaction his or her comments will elicit from the other person. This combined with emotional outbursts or hot temper can lead to failed interpersonal relationships at home or in the workplace.

Emotional outbursts and difficulty controlling one's temper are sometimes seen. **Temper outbursts** may be the result of frustration with oneself or others who do not understand the implications of having ADD. Impatience with others may also be seen in the adult with ADD and cause these emotional outbursts. In some instances, there is a tendency to overreact to small stimuli.

Low frustration tolerance and **poor self esteem** are two of the secondary symptoms of ADD. Aggressiveness, per se, is not a component of ADD. Jan Loney and her co-workers have done an excellent job in separating this trait from others present in ADD and showing that there is a separate outcome for adults, who as children, presented with aggressive or antisocial behaviors. Adults with ADD can, however, exhibit periods of depression that begin in adolescence and have a greater than average tendency to alcohol and/or drug abuse.

Adults with ADD have a greater **need for change and physical motion**. Some adults describe an inability to sit still, or the feeling that they will fall asleep if they are not allowed to move around. These symptoms can cause problems if a career choice which takes these traits into consideration is not made. The individual with these specific needs would be better suited to employment that allows him to move around to multiple job sites or change projects frequently. A desk job indoors in the same office location may prove disastrous.

Symptoms of ADD definitely interfere academically, and there is a consequent tendency for individuals with ADD to achieve less than siblings or other family members either academically or professionally. It is interesting to note that ADD is accompanied by specific learning disabilities in many individuals. The adult with ADD frequently reports difficulty with reading. These problems result both from lack of concentration and from difficulty persevering at the task. Likewise, writing which requires sustained attention and organization can be a problem. Inappropriate word choices or word-retrieval problems in reports, presentations, or conversations are seen and are most likely the result of both anxiety and attentional problems.

Prolonged effective listening is also a problem for adults with ADD. The ability to concentrate on auditorily-presented information is impaired, and there is a tendency to "tune out" during lectures or presentations. Directions and essential bits of information are frequently missed. This can also present problems during work-related seminars or workshops. In addition, the adult with ADD tends to interrupt others during conversation or to always have his own agenda, again resulting from poor listening skills.

Difficulties with the arousal mechanisms in the brain may also cause problems with sleep/awake cycles and the person with ADD may exhibit sleep disorders. This person may need little sleep or have trouble falling asleep. Sometimes they report difficulty staying awake if they have to sit for long periods, and narcolepsy (a sleep disorder) can be seen.

However, all is not necessarily negative; there are positive traits often seen in individuals with ADD. They have high levels of energy and intensity when interested. Individuals with ADD can also be very creative with lots of good ideas. Many ADD adults are good looking; many have a strong intuitive knowledge of others and empathy for them. Frequently, the deficits discussed above are matched by equally remarkable talents. An individual with poor social listening skills may also have a talent for writing. An individual with poor administrative skills may make an excellent sales person. The intensity which is characteristic of many ADD individuals and which may interfere with the ability to do routine paperwork may also result in a superlative dedication to the most important aspects of the job. When we can find a good match between the ADD adult and his work, and when proper treatment is undertaken, ADD individuals display some of the skills which are most important and desirable in an employee. Properly channeled, these qualities can lead to significant contributions in the workplace and in life.

C. CAUSES

What causes ADD, and what can be done about it?

ADD is a neurobiological condition. Although over the past two decades much research has been focused on trying to understand this condition, no single defect has been found to explain all of the symptoms of ADD. In order to look at the complex range of attentional, behavioral and emotional manifestations, we must look both at the anatomy and the biochemistry of neurotransmission in the brain.

The brain is composed of networks of individual cells called neurons. These neurons manufacture and release special chemical messengers called neurotransmitters. There are over 30 known substances that act as neurotransmitters, with many more postulated. These neurotransmitters include dopamine, norepinphrine, epinephrine, serotonin, and many more. Symptoms such as depression, sleep disorders, decreased attentiveness, and over and under arousal have all been related to actions of these neurotransmitters in the brain. New non-invasive technology has allowed for speculation about the various areas of the brain and their importance in relation to certain symptoms of ADD.

Frontal lobe and subcortical structures may be the source of the various behavioral and cognitive symptoms seen in ADD. The frontal lobes and their association with the ability to handle sequentially-received information and to organize and plan for attainment of future goals is felt to be affected in ADD. This ability is usually referred to as the **executive function** role of the frontal lobes. The basic elements of the executive function include the ability to initiate, sustain, inhibit, and shift attention. Higher executive functions include the ability to plan, organize and strategize. Self-monitoring is also a higher executive function. Dysfunction in the frontal lobes can therefore lead to problems in the areas of attention, production, and/or cognition. Research has also linked the frontal lobes, particularly the prefrontal cortex, with the limbic system, and thus to problems with motivation and emotional lability.

Using some of the newer technology, we now have studies that actually look at the functioning of brains of adults with ADD. Dr. Alan Zametkin first published his studies from the National Institutes of Mental Health in November, 1990 in the <u>New England Journal of Medicine</u>. In his study, he measured glucose metabolism in the brains of adults with histories of hyperactivity in childhood who continued to have symptoms as adults. Each adult was also the biologic parent of a hyperactive child. Results indicated that glucose metabolism in the brain was lower in adults with hyperactivity than normal controls. Among the areas of greatest reduction in metabolism were the premotor cortex and the superior prefrontal cortex, the area responsible for control of attention and motor activity.

D. TREATMENT

1. MEDICATION

While ADD cannot be "cured", adults with its symptoms can be helped. Many are now commonly seeking treatment to improve overall performance and job/life satisfaction. Education, proper diagnosis, and treatment are the keys to successfully addressing the issues that arise. Medication and other treatments are proving as successful in the workplace as in life. Stimulant medications such as methylphenidate (Ritalin) and dextroamphetamine (Dexedrine) have been found to be very effective, even in adults, in treating the symptoms of ADD.

These stimulant medications are found to improve attention span and concentration and to decrease impulsivity and distractibility, resulting in improved performance. Methylphenidate (Ritalin) is the most commonly used medication for ADD. Approximately 85% of individuals who take stimulant medication take this drug. (It is interesting to note that methylphenidate has long been used in the treatment of narcolepsy and has more recently been used in the treatment of clinical depression, both of which conditions have been sometimes found to coexist with ADD.) Dextroamphetamine (Dexedrine) is also used, particularly in adults. These medications are available in several dosage strengths, and both long and short-acting preparations. They both have side effects in some individuals, particularly anorexia (loss of appetite), weight loss, irritability, abdominal pain, and insomnia. Overmedication can result in impaired cognitive functioning. It is therefore important that these medications be prescribed and be monitored by a knowledgeable physician. Possible addiction and psychological dependence on these medications has been studied, but there is no evidence demonstrating any increased incidence of these problems in individuals being treated for ADD.

Other medications are also used to treat the symptoms of ADD. These include the tricyclic antidepressants, which, although not as effective as the stimulants, can have additional beneficial effects. Fluoxetine (Prozac) is also an antidepressant but is gaining use in the treatment of many other conditions. It is not used primarily for the core symptoms of ADD but can be useful in treating some of the related symptoms of depression or anxiety. Clonidine (Catapres) is an alpha 2 noradrenergic agonist, medicine previously used for high blood pressure but now used for many other conditions. It has also been used in the treatment of Tourette's Syndrome, obsessive compulsive disorder, ADD, and aggression. In addition, it has also recently proven effective in the treatment of migraines and nicotine withdrawal. This medicine is felt to work in ADD by decreasing arousal and is useful in treating the overaroused, hypervigilant individual.

2. OTHER TREATMENTS

The treatment of ADD requires a comprehensive program that addresses all of the individual's needs. This necessitates medical, educational, psychological, and behavioral interventions. Assistance from both mental health and medical professionals as well as educational specialists and career counsellors may be required. The individual with ADD goes through many stages as he learns about his disorder. The medications discussed above are not the only answers, but while medication does not cure the disorder, it can certainly reduce many of the symptoms. However, it is important to emphasize that other treatments should be used in conjunction with medication to assure the most positive outcome.

Psychotherapy and supportive counseling can play important roles in dealing with not only the symptoms of ADD but also the secondary emotional and social problems they exhibit. The adult with ADD needs to learn new patterns of behaviors and new approaches to situations. In addition, family members should be considered and may need to be included in counseling sessions.

Career counseling is critical for the individual in seeking appropriate employment. A knowledgeable career counselor can be of assistance in designing helpful strategies and requesting accommodations that are suited to the individual's needs. Personality testing and interest testing can assist in developing a career profile based on the strengths of each individual. A good career match can be most fulfilling and aid in unlocking some of the untapped potential possessed by the individual despite his ADD.

E. SUMMARY

Attention deficit disorder occurs in 5% to 10% of the general population. It is a very treatable disorder. Outcomes can be improved, and with adaptations, individuals can direct their own lives towards achievable, realistic goals. Employer, family, and other social supports, combined with a willingness of the individual to advocate for himself, are key elements in achieving success.

2.

WHAT ARE LEARNING DISABILITIES?

**The Editors
and
Dale S. Brown**

A. TYPES

This question does not have an easy answer. We will first state what a learning disability is not, before taking on the more complex task of defining the term.

A learning disability is **not** an emotional disturbance, mental retardation or sensory impairment. It is not a visible disability. It is not the result of environmental deprivation, inadequate parenting or poor teaching. It is not curable. Finally, it is not easy to understand.

It should be noted that there have been predecessor terms for specific learning disabilities over the years. These include dyslexia, minimal brain damage, minimal brain dysfunction and hyperactivity.

In this Chapter, we will deal with three types of definitions: practical, medical and legal. All are important in understanding learning disabilities. The governing definition for legal entitlement is the legal definition. It is important to understand that the term "learning disability" encompasses a multitude of specific deficits, each presenting in its own way and each requiring its own accommodations in the workplace as in life.

1. PRACTICAL

Practically speaking, a learning disability is a disability of neurological origin that impacts on specific areas of learning and behavior in an otherwise competent individual. These areas may include input, output and processing of information. There are many kinds of learning disabilities. Individuals may have one or more specific disabilities. Here is a general description of the various kinds.

- A sequencing disorder is a difficulty with the order of a series of things. It may lead to problems with prioritizing, organizing, doing mathematics and following instructions.

- Language disorders are difficulties with receptive language (understanding and remembering) or with expressive language, whether oral or in writing.

- Visual perceptual and visual motor disorders are difficulties with processing information visually, thus leading to problems with reading, spelling and writing, especially letters that look alike (such as b and d). This may also impact on activities requiring this skill, such as ball sports.

- A memory disorder is a difficulty retrieving certain information from memory within a reasonable time.

- Gross motor and fine motor disorders interfere with coordination. A problem with fine motor coordination could lead to difficulty with handwriting.

- An attention disorder is a difficulty in initiating and maintaining focus. It frequently is accompanied by other specific learning disabilities. Individuals with this disorder may exhibit inconsistency, impulsivity and overactivity. They may mistakenly be termed "unmotivated" or unwilling to comply with demands. See Chapter 1.

These specific learning disabilities may make it difficult for an individual to learn, work or behave in the manner that ordinarily would be expected. The impact of learning and attention disabilities may vary from day to day and situation to situation. This further complicates understanding of these disabilities by the individual and others. The variability of impact may sometimes be misunderstood and lead to an incorrect view that lesser performance is always the result of lack of motivation. As indicated above, specific disabilities may impact on the many areas of functioning, including: reading, arithmetic, spelling, writing, speaking in an organized manner, dealing with abstract concepts, sequencing, organizing, managing time, gross motor or fine motor coordination, compliant behavior, initiating and maintaining focus, handling change in routine and coping with disappointment.

Specific learning disabilities may affect 5% to 10% of the population. These disabilities may cause particular problems in the workplace.

Individuals with visual perceptual problems may have difficulty telling the difference between visually similar things, such as picking out the right can from a number of cans lined up on a shelf or the right telephone number from a series of numbers on a page.

A person with an auditory discrimination problem may have trouble discriminating the difference between sounds that he hears, such as "nineteen" and "ninety." An auditory perceptual problem may lead to difficulty taking in and acting upon oral instructions.

People with difficulty taking in information through the sense of touch may have difficulty feeling the difference between xerox paper and high quality bond paper, or difficulty judging the right amount of pressure needed to bend a plastic wire without breaking it. They may not like being touched by other people, even in fun.

Some individuals have difficulty with being aware of the passage of time and with relating things to be accomplished to a segment of time needed to do so. They may be late to work frequently, or, if their jobs involve moving from site to site, they may spend too much time at one and not enough at another.

Perceptual disabilities of various types and attention deficits not only cause difficulty in particular work tasks but may cause problems in getting along with others. For example, individuals with these disabilities may not interpret body language correctly. Such an individual might persist in talking on a topic when the body language of his co workers displays their boredom or might fail to distinguish between a polite, strained smile and a happy smile. There may be a tendency to take everything literally, the underlying meaning of a statement having been overlooked because so much work went into absorbing the words of the statement. There may be difficulty picking up on the unspoken and more subtle rules of the workplace especially those that apply generally, rather than to the core tasks of the job.

Whatever his specific disabilities, when the individual with learning disabilities enters the world of employment, he may find that he is not able to secure the jobs he would most like and for which he feels in some ways qualified. Even the process of applying for a job places demands on him in what are often his weakest areas of functioning. It is a new situation. He must rapidly process what he hears on the telephone, sees in the newspaper and encounters in an interview. He is called upon to find the prospective employer's office, bring necessary information with him, answer sometimes unanticipated questions, and appear appropriate throughout. In addition to all of these challenges, he must consider whether to disclose his disability, whether to seek accommodations on testing, if any, and finally what accommodations, if any, he should request of his employer on the job.

Once on the job, he must handle the core tasks of the job as well as the many other facets of his job in the broad sense. His interpersonal skills must be used in a wide variety of contexts: in dealings with his supervisor, relating to peers, handling customers/clients, and dealing with related personnel such as security, garage, training and the personnel office. He must do his best to pick up on subtle cues and respond appropriately.

If he gets into difficulty on the job, he must seek to talk his way out of problems and provide reassurances that he can do the job. If all of these efforts are not sufficient, and he must leave the job, he must bring to bear all of his efforts to leave on the best possible terms. However hurt or angry he may feel, he must remain focused on his goals and move forward to the next job.

He must try to learn from setbacks. A job that has not worked well for him may be an indicator that he must evaluate again what type of job is the best match for him. Hopefully, he will be able to realize that success in the workplace is an overall determination and not defined by any one job experience. As Winston Churchill observed "Success is moving from failure to failure without loss of enthusiasm." By maintaining his enthusiasm and believing in himself, he will eventually contribute talents and derive rewards in the workplace.

2. MEDICAL

Medical literature lists several types of conditions which are (or may be) considered learning disabilities. These are 1] academic skills disorders 2] learning disorders 3] motor skills disorders 4] social skills disorders and 5] some behavior disorders, e.g. attention deficit disorder.

The best known (and most generally agreed on) learning disability is dyslexia, and to this is commonly added other deficiencies in reading, writing, mathematics and spelling. Collectively, these are called "academic skills disorders" by the American Psychiatric Association in its Diagnostic and Statistical Manual of Mental Disorders (DSM-III-R). THE MERCK MANUAL (15th Ed. 1987) uses the term "learning disability" to cover "problems in reading, arithmetic, spelling, and written expression." THE MERCK MANUAL (15th Ed. 1987) at 1975

But learning *disabilities* are not the only learning *problems*. The DSM-III-R identifies the following additional problems ("developmental disorders" to use its terms): 1] "language and speech disorders" 2] "motor skills disorders" and 3] "disruptive behavior disorders." THE MERCK MANUAL (15th Ed. 1987) terms language and speech disorders "learning disorders" which is a far broader term covering virtually any learning impairment and includes both learning disabilities and more pervasive disorders such as autism and mental retardation. THE MERCK MANUAL (15th Ed. 1987) at 1975

The final categories of learning disability are those of behavior and social skills disorders. In LEARNING DISABILITIES: A REPORT TO THE U.S. CONGRESS, Interagency Committee on Learning Disabilities (1987), the Committee defined "learning disabilities" to include 1] specific developmental disabilities of reading, writing, and mathematics 2] developmental language disorders 3] social skills deficits and 4] attention deficit disorder. The Report states that ADD should be a "central focus" of any discussion of learning disabilities because ADD often coexists in individuals with learning disabilities and complicates their diagnoses and treatment. The DSM-III-R lists Attention Deficit Disorder and Attention Deficit Hyperactivity Disorder. (Note: the DSM-III-R also lists conduct disorder as a behavior disorder; it is not generally listed as a learning disability.)

Essentially, medical authorities disagree on 1] whether "learning disabilities" should be limited to those disorders which **primarily** impact academic skills 2] what **other** skills, such as language, speech, motor coordination, and socialization, should be considered and 3] whether behavior disorders (such as ADD) should be included. In this latter respect, some authorities consider ADD not to be a learning disability *because* it is a behavior disorder. Implicit in this view is the notion that behavior is voluntary, whereas the development of language, speech, and academic skills depend on physical or physiological causes. Others, however, view learning as so heavily dependent on attention that the supposed differences in kind among academic skills, behavior and development disorders disappear or assume insignificant proportions.

Finally, there is almost complete agreement as to what learning disabilities are **not**. They are **not** the product of 1] mental illness, 2] visual, hearing, or motor impairments, 3] mental retardation, 4] autism, 5] emotional disturbance, or 6] environmental, cultural, or economic disadvantage. Learning problems resulting from these causes may be no less serious than learning disabilities; indeed, they may be more serious. But they are disorders, disadvantages and deficits which fall into other categories than learning disabilities and pose different medical and legal issues.

The multiple meanings of the term "learning disability" might be pictured this way:

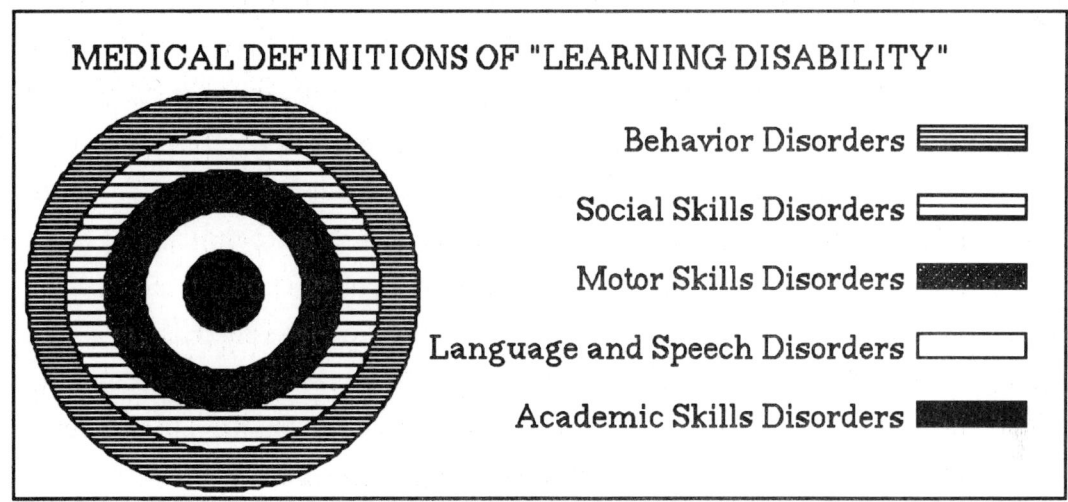

The diagram emphasizes the range of definitions from the narrow "academic skills" definition to one which includes disorders which impact on behavior, such as ADD. As you can see, it is extremely important to know how broadly the term is being used. But, as if that were not enough, we must also consider the legal definition.

3. LEGAL

The purpose of this text is to discuss attention deficit disorder and learning disabilities in the workplace. The legal definition of learning disability is important. The legal definition is not necessarily the same as the medical one. Generally speaking, the authors of the statutes we will be considering drafted them to help people and, in doing so, included many types of disabilities within the definitions. Therefore, in some cases, the legal definitions may appear to be broader than the medical ones. However, the authors of the statutes also wanted to ensure that assistance is concentrated on the truly needy and so limited relief to those persons whose lives were substantially impacted by the disorders. Finally, some statutes use medical terminology which once had meaning but is now obsolete.

The predominant legal definition, which is set forth in the Individuals With Disabilities Education Act (IDEA). 20 U. S.C. § 1401(a)(15), provides:

> (a)(15) The term 'children with specific learning disabilities' means those children who have a disorder in one or more of the basic psychological processes involved in understanding or in using language, spoken or written, which disorder may manifest itself in imperfect ability to listen, think, speak, read, write, spell or do mathematical calculations. Such disorders include such conditions as perceptual disabilities, brain injury, minimal brain dysfunction, dyslexia, and developmental aphasia. Such term does not include children who have learning problems which are primarily the result of visual, hearing, or motor disabilities, of mental retardation, of emotional disturbance, or of environmental, cultural, or economic disadvantage.

Other statutes, such as the Rehabilitation Act of 1973 and the Americans with Disabilities Act, essentially adopt this definition of a learning disability. Note, however, that they extend their protections only to those learning disabilities which "substantially limit one or more major life activities" of the individual affected by it. (For that matter, the IDEA itself only protects children with specific learning disabilities "who, by reason thereof need special education and related services.") As a result, the legal definition includes some but not all the medical elements and adds some elements which are not medically important.

4. CONCLUSION

In considering learning disabilities in the workplace, it will be necessary to work with the practical, medical and legal definitions. In asserting legal rights in the workplace, the legal definition will be of <u>central</u> importance.

B. CAUSES

The causes of learning disabilities (other than those resulting from physical injury, e.g. head injury, ingestion of lead paint, etc.) are unknown. The probable causes of learning disabilities lie in the physiology and operation of the brain and neurological system. Heredity may be a factor. Learning is a process which consists of at least two activities, the learning of skills and the learning of facts. Brain structure, memory circuits and synapses are all immediately involved in the learning process, and it is reasonable to assume that learning disabilities result from interferences in the operation of those mechanisms. The Interagency Committee on Learning Disabilities concluded that to understand learning and learning disabilities one must study:

> • Key brain regions: the location of those regions in the brain associated with the storage, retrieval, and processing of different types of memory.
>
> • Memory 'circuits' in brain: the characteristics of the circuitries contained within learning-related brain structures and how these characteristics are linked to the phenomenologies observed at the other levels of analysis.
>
> • Synaptic mechanisms: the nature of the stable modifications that actually encode memory, and the types of mechanisms that produce those modifications. LEARNING DISABILITIES: A REPORT TO THE U.S. CONGRESS Interagency Committee on Learning Disabilities (1987) at 121

According to the Committee, the probable causes of learning disabilities are physiological interruptions in the learning process:

> What are the possible neurobiological causes of learning disabilities? Clearly, learning depends on the proper operation of defined circuits that transfer the information and ultimately store it in a form accessible for retrieval. The substrate often appears to involve molecular changes in ex-

isting connections, or as more recent data indicate, actual formation (turnover) of new synapses.

What are the steps where learning has "weak links? Neuropsychologists have amply documented the crucial roles played by general body and brain states such as arousal, motivation, attention, etc. Learning does not occur without a prior focusing of attention and without appropriate motivation. Deficiencies in these states can be expected to have powerful consequences on early learning abilities, and it is likely that disturbances do occur. Perturbations in the machinery that controls arousal, for example, are not uncommon in children who are often present as a hyperkinetic syndrome. Brain states are also known to exert a powerful influence over the body's endocrine system, and hormone levels in turn have been linked to the strengths of the memory trace. LEARNING DISABILITIES: A REPORT TO THE U.S. CONGRESS Interagency Committee on Learning Disabilities (1987) at 130

C. SUMMARY

This Chapter is about learning disabilities, a term which has numerous meanings. **Practical** discussions examine how specific learning disabilities impact upon functioning in life in general and in the workplace in particular. **Medical** definitions start with "academic skills disorders" such as dyslexia, and vary to the extent that they include other disabilities. There is not complete unanimity on 1] whether "learning disabilities" should be limited to those disorders which **primarily** impact academic skills 2] what other skills, such as language, speech, motor coordination, and socialization should be considered and 3] whether disorders that impact on behavior (such as ADD) should be included. The **legal** definition of a "learning disability" is: "a disorder in one or more of the basic psychological processes involved in understanding or in using language, spoken or written, which disorder may manifest itself in imperfect ability to listen, think, speak, read, write, spell or do mathematical calculations." In addition, the "learning disability" must be one "that substantially limits one or more of the major life activities" of the individual who has it.

Learning disabilities are information input, output and processing difficulties, most probably with a neurobiological etiology. These disabilities occur in 5% to 10% of the population. Heredity may be an important factor. Individuals with learning disabilities have special needs which can usually be met by providing remediation and accommodations.

3.

STRATEGIES AND ACCOMMODATIONS

Kathleen Nadeau, Ph. D.

A. OVERVIEW

Adulthood can provide an individual who has struggled with learning and/or attentional problems throughout his life with opportunities that did not exist in school. As adults, we all have a much broader range of choices than in childhood, allowing the selection of occupations which emphasize personal strengths and minimize requirements for the performance of tasks which are personally difficult.

In this Chapter, we will discuss how to go about making good career choices and some situations to avoid. We list some reasonable accommodations which can be provided by an employer, and, most importantly, we discuss many strategies to improve performance on the job. Be aware that there are large differences among adults with ADD and LD. Not everything which follows applies to all situations. This Chapter is designed for use as part of a self-evaluation process.

B. POTENTIAL PROBLEM SITUATIONS TO CONSIDER

There are a number of factors to consider in selecting the type of job for which you may be best suited. What follows is addressed to those who have not yet selected a particular profession or area of expertise and those who, by preference or necessity have undertaken to rethink their initial decisions in this matter.

1. Jobs with high requirements for paperwork and record keeping tend to be very difficult for adults with attention deficits or learning disabilities.

2. Jobs which have managerial and supervisory responsibilities are often a poor match if you have difficulty with details, with organization, and with shifting from one activity to another.

3. In general, high stress jobs with expectations for rapid performance are less desirable.

4. Disorganized, poorly managed workplace environments should be avoided.

5. Working under a rigid, demanding or critical supervisor can be very destructive for an adult with ADD and LD.

6. Jobs with an expectation for rapid learning are hard for the adult with ADD/LD. These adults need to be able to learn in a learning environment which suits them - whether this means at a slower pace, with hands-on instruction or with more individualized instruction.

C. POSITIVE TRAITS

While it is important to consider traits in adults with ADD which may negatively impact job performance, it is also essential to give attention to positive traits which may be associated with ADD. Some adults with ADD make excellent sales people, promoters, and lobbyists due to their social skills and boundless energy. Still others are blessed with an endless flow of creative ideas and associations which make them marvelous brain-stormers and catalysts. Many hyperactive adults use their boundless energy very effectively in entrepreneurial activities. Other adults with ADD respond superbly to situations calling for crisis intervention or immediate problem-solving.

Likewise, for adults with learning disabilities (and remember, many adults with ADD also have LD), there are often strengths which more than offset areas of difficulty. In fact, some neurologists believe that a deficit, or learning disability, in one area is the "price" paid for a great gift or strength in another area. Adults with learning disabilities often make superb employees because they have long ago learned that they need to work smarter and harder to compensate for their areas of disability.

D. THE POWER OF PERSONALITY

No person with a disability is defined solely by that disability. The same is true of learning disabilities and attention deficit disorder. Although they are important considerations when you make a career choice, it is equally important to consider your personality type. Are you an introvert or an extrovert? Are you a creative person, an idea person, an innovator? Do you like a highly structured job in which you know exactly what is expected of you, or do you prefer a job which offers freedom and independence? What are your values? What is most important to you in a job - challenge, convenience, high income, prestige, flexible hours? Do you prefer to work outside, to move from one job site to another or to work in an office environment? Would you prefer to work out of your home? It may be helpful to spend time with a job counselor to explore all of these issues. It can also be extremely helpful to take a personality test such as the Myers-Briggs Type Inventory. Once your personality type has been determined, your counselor can give you ideas about jobs most suited to people with your personality type.

E. STRATEGIES AND ACCOMMODATIONS

As you prepare to enter the workplace, or to re-evaluate your role in the workplace, be positive and consider the following:

1] suggested areas for **skill enhancement** through courses or tutoring
2] **reasonable accommodations** to be requested from your employer
3] **compensatory strategies** you will need on the job.

1. Skill Enhancement

Skill enhancement might mean working with a tutor who is skilled in teaching adults with learning problems to improve your writing or math ability. It might involve taking a class at the local community college to increase your knowledge level in an area which interests you. It could even involve a return to school for a degree in the area for which you seem best suited.

You might need to develop certain technical skills which you have avoided due to your learning problems. You may need more individualized training, or training at a slower pace, as you learn to operate new equipment or to use a new software package.

2. Reasonable Accommodations

Accommodations are ways in which your employer can assist you to maximize your functioning at work. While specific accommodations are important, the most important accommodation factors are intangible. They involve a supportive, flexible attitude on the part of your supervisor or employer, and a positive, motivated, and pro-active attitude on your part. If these attitudes are in place, then other accommodations are more likely to fall into place. While you read through the list of accommodations which follows, keep in mind that it is ultimately your responsibility, not the responsibility of your employer, to find a good job match for yourself and to learn strategies to aid your ability to perform your job.

The Job Accommodations Network (JAN), a service of the President's Committee on Employment of People with Disabilities, was established in 1984 to provide information about job accommodations to individuals with all types of disabilities. Reasonable accommodations for ADD and LD adults, suggested by JAN and by others include:

1. A private office or non-distracting work-space.

2. If space restrictions cannot allow a private office, then the provision of temporary quiet space for tasks which demand high concentration.

3. Allowing the employee to do some work at home.

4. Provision of flex time. Distractible individuals are more productive during "off-hours" when fewer co-workers are present.

5. Day-planner computer software to assist in organization and planning, with visual and auditory alarms as reminder to improve time management.

6. Assistance in setting up a more organized filing system.

7. Video or audio tape equipment to assist with auditory memory deficits.

8. Checklists to provide structure in multi-stage tasks.

9. Giving instructions slowly and clearly.

10. Allowing the employee to tape record meetings.

11. Writing down instructions or communications so the employee has a written record.

12. Excusing the individual from non-essential tasks.

13. Job restructuring to better suit the individual's strengths.

14. More frequent performance appraisals.

15. Reassignment to a vacant position which better matches the individual's strengths.

16. Extra clerical support.

17. Providing a manual or handbook in writing, with highlights to clearly outline rules, regulations and expectations.

18. Providing a bulletin board for announcements.

19. Providing set routines and schedules wherever possible.

20. Clearly defining lines of authority.

21. A supervisor who can serve as a "funnel" when task assignments come from multiple sources.

22. Clearly defining mechanisms for communication between employee and supervisor.

23. Repeat advance notice of changes in routine: whether it be holidays, pay schedules, or schedule of work hours.

24. Keeping written communication simple and clear.

26. Breaking down tasks into smaller units and providing prompts for transition from one step to the next.

27. Providing information in both the visual and auditory modes.

28. Using graphics to illustrate projects.

29. Using time-line charts to help the employee visualize the flow of a complicated multi-phase project.

Note that these accommodations are reasonable in the sense that they are compensatory actions which an employer might want to take to ensure that the talents of an individual with ADD/LD can be used effectively in the workplace. As such, they represent approaches which should commend themselves to sophisticated managers in particular cases. They are not necessarily the minimum "reasonable accommodations" whose provision is required by law.

3. Compensatory Strategies

Below is an extensive, but not exhaustive, list of strategies which may be useful to you. No individual will need to make use of them all. After carefully evaluating the areas in which you experience difficulty, you should then choose the strategies which you feel might work best for you. These are tools which you can choose to use. Rather than feeling that you are a victim of a set of disabilities, you need to approach these strategies with the attitude that they will assist you in taking charge of your situation to turn it to your best advantage.

■ *Hyperactivity*

1. Look for work in a job which allows a high degree of physical movement.

2. If you are currently employed at a job which requires prolonged desk work or work at a computer terminal, take frequent breaks which allow movement. A simple walk to the water fountain and back every 20 to 30 minutes will be helpful.

3. Make sure you arrange for activity on your coffee breaks and lunch breaks. Go for a walk rather than getting a cup of coffee.

4. Bring your lunch so that you can spend the lunch hour walking or exercising in some other fashion.

5. The more sedentary your work is, the more important it will be to engage in strenuous physical activity in your after-work hours.

6. If you are considering a job change, look for a job that allows you to be on your feet more. Work which allows movement from room to room at work, which calls for frequent interpersonal interaction, or which allows you to travel from one job site to another will be more suited to your temperament.

7. Work which requires participation in long meetings or which consists primarily of sedentary detailed desk work is less suited to your needs.

■ *Distractibility*

1. Set aside periods of your day when you will not be interrupted except in case of emergencies. Let your supervisor and co-workers know how important it is for you to have uninterrupted time.

2. Fight internal distractions through scheduling your intensive work in time-limited chunks. Daydreaming is more likely if you have set aside a long period of time in which to work on a task.

3. If internal distraction is severe, you may need to carefully analyze how suited you are to the work you have been assigned. Daydreaming is much more likely when doing tedious or low-interest work.

4. If you are distracted, not by daydreaming, but by a rapid flow of ideas which are tangentially related to the project at hand or are related to other work projects, develop the habit of writing down the intruding thought. This will allow you to return to it efficiently, when appropriate, but also allows you to continue with the immediate task.

5. A rapid flow of ideas, distracting you from the issue at hand, can present difficulties when talking in meetings. If you have a tendency to ramble or to become tangential, make brief notes about what you want to say and refer to them.

6. You may also find yourself distracted in meetings as you think of comments you would like to make while listening to someone else speak. To keep yourself from being so distracted by your own thoughts that you cannot focus on the speaker, write your ideas down briefly, so that you can refer to them when the time comes for you to speak. This approach will help you be seen as someone who is focused and organized, rather than appearing to be someone who is "always going off half-cocked."

7. If you catch yourself becoming distracted, i.e. returning phone calls, opening mail, reading a work related document unrelated to the task in which

you are engaged, learn to catch yourself, consciously stop, and re-engage in the previous task.

8. For highly distractible individuals, an orderly work-space is highly important. Do not surround yourself with piles of paperwork and post-it notes.

9. If your work space is messy, don't make the desk clearing process into a major project which distracts you even further from your task. Simply clear off your desk of all papers other than those on which you are working, even if it means putting piles of documents, unfiled, in an out-of-sight placement. Then schedule, as an assigned task, a time to re-organize your work space.

■ *Organization*

1. If organization and follow-through are weak points for you, try to work as a team with someone for whom these skills are a strength. An enthusiastic, creative adult with ADD often makes an excellent partner for an individual who may be less creative, but better organized.

2. Develop the habit of setting aside 15 minutes at the beginning of each day for planning. This will give you an overview of your day and help you function in an organized fashion throughout the day.

3. Poor follow-through is often related to distractibility. As you are engaged in one prolonged task, another idea comes along which captures your interest. You need to catch yourself and go back to the original task. Use new interests or projects as a reward for completion of previous projects.

4. For some adults with ADD, work on long complicated projects is simply incompatible with their short-term interests. If lack of follow-through is a major difficulty for you in your current position, you may want to avoid long term projects when choosing your next job. There are many jobs which involve immediate or short-term issues.

5. If at all possible, avoid jobs in which you are assigned work by a number of different people. Such a position is difficult, even for persons with good organizational skills.

■ Time Management

1. Learn to think pro-actively rather than re-actively. Plan your day rather than reacting to events, impulses and moods.

2. Don't overschedule your day.

3. Build slack time into your day. This will allow you to remain unstressed and on-time, even when inevitable interruptions occur.

4. Break large tasks into chunks. Give yourself concrete assignments to complete by specified times.

5. Keep your daily schedule with you at all times. When you take on a new task, schedule it, i.e., don't just say "I'll call you," or "I'll get it to you later this week," without scheduling an actual time to complete that task. If you can't assign the task an exact time, then put it on your "to do" list on a specific day.

6. If you tend to lose track of time when you are engaged in conversation or in intensive work, set a timer to beep at the time you need to terminate the conversation or task. Some adults with ADD become so engrossed that they cannot remember to check their watches.

7. Learn not to say "yes" when you need to say "no." While hard work, motivation and willingness to accommodate the needs of your supervisor and co-workers are positive traits, you need to set reasonable limits so that you are not overly stressed, frequently running late or missing deadlines. Develop the habit of saying "let me think about it in terms of my other commitments" rather than reflexively saying "yes."

8. Learn to say "no" to last minute impulses unless they are true emergencies. Many ADD adults are chronically late due to a series of impulses to take care of some brief task that occurs to them as they are on their way out the door to do something else.

9. Remind yourself as you are leaving for a scheduled meeting not to get caught in hallway conversations which will throw off your best laid plans.

10. Plan to be early. Take some work or reading material with you so that the time isn't wasted.

11. Learn to end phone calls or conversations a few minutes early. Ending a conversation often takes longer than you had planned, making you late for your next commitment. Always leave yourself a little leeway.

■ *Procrastination*

1. Give yourself deadlines.

2. Build in rewards for yourself. (When I finish this letter I'll go downstairs for a cup of coffee.)

3. Make commitments to others. You are less likely to procrastinate if you have made a commitment to someone about when you will complete the work.

4. Ask yourself if your job involves too many tasks which you simply don't enjoy, have difficulty doing or find tedious. Severe procrastination may be a sign of a poor job match.

■ *Low Frustration Tolerance*

1. Try to analyze the situations which recur at work that are the most stressful for you. Analyze whether there is a way to reduce or minimize such occurrences.

2. Take your frustration level seriously. Don't wait until you "can't take it" before you leave the frustrating situation.

3. Try to avoid working for intense, high stress organizations or individuals.

4. Work at developing relaxation techniques to use at the office. Some techniques involve muscle relaxation or guided imagery.

5. Long hours and time pressure will increase your tendency to feel stressed. Try to avoid these situations whenever possible.

6. Look for work which allows autonomy, which lets you set your own pace and which allows you time alone.

■ *Interpersonal Conflicts On The Job*

1. Try to analyze whether you can see patterns in the conflicts you have had over the years. There may be some issues you need to explore in counseling.

2. Some adults with ADD "don't know when to stop." They keep on at something, missing non-verbal cues from others indicating discomfort. If this is a pattern for you, you may need to learn to recognize and catch yourself in this pattern in order to minimize this tendency.

3. If you have been called stubborn or argumentative, practice active listening - that is, pay attention and try to understand fully what is being said to you rather than immediately responding with a negative or contradictory remark.

4. If being hot-tempered plays a role in your interpersonal conflicts on the job, you may need to become a better judge of your mood and frustration level in order to avoid interpersonal confrontations. Develop an "early warning system" to judge your mood and escape the situation temporarily before you explode. Learn to cool off before re-engaging in discussion or negotiations.

5. Work which allows a high degree of autonomy and personal freedom may be best for individuals who find they have little patience or tolerance for the inevitable problems which arise when working with others.

■ *Prioritization*

1. Don't just dive in. Develop the habit of planning your day and doing your plan.

2. Stop and catch yourself when you fall into the reactive mode. As a reactor you have abandoned your set of priorities, allowing a set of random events or the priorities of others to take precedence over your goals.

3. Learn to categorize tasks in A-B-C fashion:

    A - has to be done today.

    B - would like to get done today.

    C - will do today if all A's and B's are completed.

4. Catch yourself if you impulsively say "yes" to a request without consideration of your established priorities. Learn to say "I'd like to, let me think about it."

■ *Memory*

1. Bring tape recorders to important meetings and seminars.

2. Take notes during the meetings you are recording. If there is a point of particular importance, reference the "counter" on your tape recorder so that you can easily fast-forward to this point on the tape for review. This prevents the need to re-listen to the entire meeting or seminar to refer to particular points.

3. Take notes during meetings, even brief casual meetings with your supervisor or co-worker. Don't ever rely on memory. Always keep a written record of things you or your co-worker have agreed to do, or which have been communicated to you.

4. After important meetings or agreements, provide other individuals with a written copy of your interpretation of agreements made so that you can double check for accuracy.

5. Keep your daytimer with you at all times. Write brief notes regarding decisions and commitments you make. Don't rely on your memory until you get back to your office. Write it down, just as if you were a sales person taking an order. If you are making a commitment, write that commitment down on a specific day and time at which you plan to keep that commitment - don't just relegate the commitment to your never-ending "to do" list.

■ *Reading Problems*

1. When you have lengthy manuals or reports to read and review, it is helpful to learn "pre-reading strategies" to help you to develop a mental framework for the information you are about to read. For example, survey the chapter before reading and turn the subheadings into an item list while reading. When you have an overall picture of what the manual or report encompasses, then go back, section by section, reviewing each topic. Reading aloud or taking notes can enhance your concentration and your reading comprehension.

2. In order to monitor your reading comprehension you should stop periodically while reading and ask yourself if you understand what you have read. If the reading is very technical or demanding you should try to paraphrase the main idea and supporting details of each paragraph after reading it.

3. To improve concentration while reading, try using a compact recorder while reading, dictating a summary of each paragraph of text and noting the important data.

4. Using a marker or highlighter when reading can assist with concentration and comprehension.

5. In order to increase your vocabulary and reading comprehension abilities, it is helpful to read books for pleasure that are of a high interest level for you.

6. When reading is an extreme problem it may be best to have a computer with a scanner which can scan and read aloud written material to you.

■ *Writing Difficulties*

1. It is essential that you develop keyboarding skills and learn to use a word processing program with a spell check capability.

2. You can improve your written expression skills by learning to generate ideas and then organize the ideas into an outline prior to beginning a written assignment.

3. Even though you should have a computer with spell check and grammar check, it can also be helpful to have a co-worker who can review mechanics such as punctuation, usage, and spelling before a final document is presented.

4. If oral expression is easier for you, dictate reports or memos and then transcribe them yourself or have them transcribed for you. After this stage, you can work from a draft to make corrections or additions to your dictation.

5. Don't get caught up in perfectionism. Too many adults with writing difficulties almost "freeze" when asked to write a letter or report. Just make a rough outline and get started. It's much easier to improve a rough draft than to attempt perfection from the start.

■ Visual-Spatial Problems

1. It goes without saying that jobs which require visual-spatial skills, such as engineering, mechanics, drafting and design will be difficult. Depending upon the degree of difficulty you have in this area, you may be able to handle such tasks if they are not a major part of your job description and if you have close supervision.

2. If you experience difficulty with directionality, you may want to take extra care and extra time when you go to a new work environment to learn your way around.

3. If travel to varying job sites is required, you may need to develop special maps to aid you. Some people find it very helpful to mark the route from one job site to the next on a map using a **light**-colored magic marker (so that the marker doesn't keep you from being able to read the map names through the markings.)

4. Other people with visual-spatial difficulties move best from one location to another using visual signs or markers rather than using a map. If this is the case, you will need to do some advance planning, making a trial run in order to take notes; i.e., "go down Rt. 50 to the Exxon station and turn right, keep going until you pass the high school on your left, etc."

■ Math Problems

1. If your math disability is not extreme, you should be able to perform most of the functions required in jobs as long as they are not positions which require higher level math, such as scientific, engineering, or accounting positions.

2. Use a calculator at all times. Don't rely on yourself to do hand-written calculations.

3. If careless errors are part of your difficulty with math a "talking calculator," which is readily available at most electronics stores, may be helpful in catching your errors as you enter them into the calculator.

■ *Auditory Processing Problems*

1. Try to avoid positions which require that a significant portion of your day is spent in verbal interaction with others.

2. In important meetings, conferences or even important conversations, develop the habit of taping the proceedings.

3. For important taped conversations transcribe the tape, editing it to eliminate non-essential material, so that you have a written record of what was decided or agreed upon.

4. If you are feeling particularly "burnt out" from a long period of listening, ask others to "please get that to me in writing" rather than continuing to require yourself to listen.

5. Don't be hesitant to ask people to speak more slowly or to please repeat or rephrase what they have just said.

4. GENERAL STRATEGIES

We've just listed a large group of specific strategies which individual with learning or attentional problems might find helpful on the job. It is important for you to know that there are more general strategies or approaches, unrelated to specific disabilities, which can greatly enhance your chances for professional success. A study of highly successful adults with learning disabilities was conducted to try to identify what traits they held in common. The study found that they all shared the following **internal attributes**:

1. Each of them had a strong desire for success.

2. They were all tremendously determined to succeed.

3. Each of them expressed a powerful need for control of his own destiny and, perhaps most importantly,

4. Each of them had learned to "reframe" his learning disabilities in a more positive and productive manner.

They also shared a number of **external conditions**:

1. Most highly successful adults with learning disabilities reported they had a mentor who served as a close advisor and role model.

2. They surrounded themselves with positive, supportive people.

3. They arranged experiences strategically designed to develop or enhance their skills.

4. They were willing to seek out, appreciate and accept help appropriately from others without becoming dependent.

5. They all seemed to have a good match between their particular strengths and weaknesses and the jobs in which they were employed.

As you are working toward finding a satisfying career path, keep these success strategies in mind. No matter what is the best job match for you and no matter which particular areas of difficulty you experience, these success strategies can help you reach your goal.

F. SUMMARY

In this Chapter we've covered a range of important topics to aid you in achieving success on the job, including things to consider in choosing your next job, job pitfalls to avoid, ways that you can develop more job skills, accommodations which can be provided by your employer and strategies you can adopt to minimize problem areas in the workplace. Lastly, we outlined the results of a study of highly successful adults with learning disabilities to let you know some of the factors which led to their success. Spend the time to find a good job match. Don't let yourself become discouraged by negative messages. Surround yourself with positive and encouraging people, and be sure to give yourself positive messages too! Your chances as an adult with LD or ADD to succeed in the workplace have never been better!

4.

FINDING THE JOB

Electronic Industries Foundation Project With Industry Program

A. GETTING ORGANIZED

1. KEEPING RECORDS OF THE JOB SEARCH

Your job search is important; it should be conducted like a 40-hour a week job. This means mapping out a strategy for your search and being systematic about accomplishing the work of finding a job.

Your job search will require multiple and different types of contacts with employers; you will be preparing different kinds of letters and speaking to many different people. It is important to record each contact and the place and time it occurred. Key items to record are the names and job titles of people you meet with or talk with, the main points of the conversation, the dates those contacts took place, the companies these people are employed by, the jobs you apply for and the dates when you send any letters, resumes, samples or follow-up letters as part of the application process. It will take some discipline and practice at first to begin recording all this information regularly, but it soon will become second nature. This will help you track your progress toward your goal of employment.

2. TIME MANAGEMENT

Time management is the process by which you arrange your hours and days in order to accomplish as many tasks as efficiently as you can. Three terms are important to remember as you work to manage your time wisely: **ORGANIZE, PRIORITIZE,** and **REORGANIZE.**

First, **organize** all your tasks, those you want to accomplish as well as those you must accomplish. Then **prioritize** them according to how essential each is toward achieving your goal of employment. Focus on your goal as you arrange your schedule. To prioritize your day's activities, first make a list of everything you want to accomplish. Then, go through the list and sort each task into one of the following groups:

>   What must be done
>   What should be done
>   What would be nice to get done
>   What can wait

Grouping your activities makes the day's top priorities clear--the tasks that **must** be done. However, priorities can change and many tasks may move from the "should be done" to the "must be done" list. It is important to review and **reorganize** your list from time to time, perhaps weekly. Each person will have tasks unrelated to the job search that are also important. Ranking your priorities should be done with the job search goal in mind while allowing for other tasks that need to be accomplished from day to day.

B. THE RESUME

Your resume is the bait that can land you an interview - the first major goal of your job search. Your resume must be geared toward convincing an employer that time should be invested in meeting you.

1. DEVELOPING A RESUME WORKSHEET

With dozens, sometimes hundreds, of applicants applying for each job opening, an employer may scan your resume for less than a minute. What makes one resume stand out from another? **Preparation.** Your resume must demonstrate that your background and skills match the basic job requirements. Before you begin to write it, organize the information on paper to help you focus on those experiences and achievements, both in your career and outside work, which support your job objective.

■ Job Objective

Write one sentence to clarify your job objective - what you are looking for in a job. State what specific goal you want to achieve, (e.g. secretarial job within the medical field); **not** what you want from an employer.

■ Employment Experience

Record all full-time and part-time employment. List the dates you worked, names of employers/organizations, job titles, accomplishments, skills learned, and major responsibilities and duties. Begin with your most recent job and work backwards. If you have held many jobs, in your actual resume you may want to summarize your early experience in a single sentence.

Example: Early work experience includes payroll input and accounts receivable.

■ Education

List degrees you have earned, the institutions from which they were earned, and the dates of attendance. List the highest level of education you achieved first and end with high school. Outline special courses you have taken to upgrade or enhance skills that correlate to the job you seek. Relevant special school projects and internships also should be included, especially if you lack significant work experience. In preparing your final resume, if you wish, you may delete the dates. They indicate your age, information you are not required to give.

■ Licenses and Accreditation

List any certifications and professional licenses you possess. Include the title, issuing agency, and date of issue.

■ Military Service

List any information related to military service.

■ Volunteer Experience

Record work-related unpaid experience. Include dates, organization names, volunteer titles, accomplishments, skills learned, and major responsibilities and duties.

■ Professional Affiliations and Organization Memberships

List all professional, civic, and social organizations to which you currently belong. Record names of organizations, positions and committee assignments held, and the dates you held them.

■ Awards and Honors

List all awards that you earned either in paid or unpaid positions, in or out of school. List your grade point average if it is 3.00 or higher if you lack significant work experience.

■ Skills

List all skills that are pertinent to the job you are applying for (e.g., computer literacy, shorthand, typing speed).

2. THE ANATOMY OF A RESUME

There are three standard types of resumes: chronological, functional and combination. Based on the information on your worksheet, select the format that you believe best fits your employment history, the type of job you are seeking and your skills.

■ Chronological

This format is most frequently used in preparing a resume. It follows the history of your work experience arranged in reverse chronological order, that is it begins with your most recent job and works backwards. Each position description includes the name of the company, dates employed, job title and responsibilities. This resume style typically is used by people who have a fairly consistent work history with few gaps in employment. A sample chronological resume is presented in Appendix A.

■ Functional

This format summarizes and emphasizes qualifications, skills, abilities, and accomplishments. The functional style is more commonly used by those who have had limited employment or who have been unemployed for long periods of time, those who have changed jobs frequently, or those who wish to make a career change. The format allows you to present the job skills most relevant to the job you seek and focuses less on employment history and experience. You will find a sample of this form of resume presented in Appendix B.

■ Combination

This format is just what its name states. It combines both the chronological and functional approaches to preparing a resume. Job experiences that stress specific skills are highlighted as they relate to job objectives. This listing is followed by a chronology of how, where, and when these skills were acquired and used. A sample combination resume is presented in Appendix C.

3. Helpful Tips in Preparing a Resume

Having selected the format to use, you can now begin developing a rough draft. The following tips can help you now and as a checklist once your resume is completed.

Be accurate, clear and concise. Do not exaggerate past and current job responsibilities and accomplishments.

Have the resume neatly word processed or printed on good quality paper. While the color of the paper is not necessarily important, some recruiters recommend that paper should be off-white or white.

Carefully check your resume for spelling and grammatical errors. If possible, have two other people check your resume for grammar, spelling, content and style.

4. Achievement Words For Resumes

Use action statements and words as you prepare your resume. They attract attention and suggest motion, success, and leadership skills. Here are some examples of action-oriented statements:

Responsibilities included supervising staff, promoting and marketing services and managing budgets.

Recommended and implemented a successful department plan that led to improved staff performance and an increase in company profits.

Directed a staff of ten that received two performance awards.

Presented below are examples of achievement words that may be helpful to you in preparing your resume.

accomplished	controlled	initiated	recorded
achieved	coordinated	interviewed	recruited
actively	created	invented	referred
advised	designed	issued	reorganized
allocated	developed	led	researched
analyzed	directed	maintained	resolved
assisted	drafted	managed	reviewed
attended	enlarged	organized	scheduled
balanced	equipped	planned	sold
completed	established	prepared	studied
computed	expanded	presented	supervised
constructed	implemented	produced	supported
contracted	improved	recommended	trained

C. FINDING JOB LEADS

Getting a job requires job leads. Only 25 percent of all available jobs are advertised or offered through an agency. Furthermore, up to 75 percent of all jobs are obtained using nontraditional resources that focus on "hidden" job leads, such as friends, relatives, and co-workers. In your search for a job, you will do best by using as many job lead resources as you can.

1. RESOURCES FOR THE "HIDDEN" JOB MARKET
   (OVER HALF OF JOB SEARCH TIME)

■ Telephone Books

Look through the Yellow Pages and group companies according to what they do or make. Then match your skills with the companies most likely to need them. When you identify which organizations best suit your needs, call the person who has authority to hire (e.g., department manager, supervisor) and request an interview.

Most White Pages now include a section of Blue Pages, which list local government agencies--an additional employment option.

- **Friends, Relatives, Past Employers, and Co-Workers**

Because these individuals know you, they are important job lead sources. They may know of specific openings or may be able to recommend you to an employer.

- **Directories**

Your Chamber of Commerce may publish listings of local employers, which can be used the same way you use the Yellow Pages. Your neighborhood public library subscribes to a wide variety of local and national business and association directories. The United Way publishes the "Help Book," which lists the names of agencies that often require employees for a variety of positions.

- **Contacts**

You may decide to visit the personnel office of a company in which you are interested without first making contact by telephone. Usually, you can obtain information about the company and fill out an application form without an appointment.

- **Academic Networks**

Alumni associations, fraternities, sororities, and academic societies may have informal job networking programs to put members in touch with other members who are in careers or positions of interest. Contact your chapter or national office to find out what services are available. Members may be willing to talk with you about your job search and your goals.

- **Newspapers**

Search the general news for information about new or expanding companies or organizations that may need employees.

2. Resources for the "Visible" Job Market
   (Less than Half of Job Search Time)

■ Newspapers Again

Read the want ads. Learn to locate those most appropriate for your skills and interests. Be sure to act on want ads as soon as possible (within a week)!

■ State and Local Employment Services

Use state and local employment services. They may have various names. A few examples are: "Job Service Registration" and "Department of Employment Services".

Also consult with the City or County Division of Vocational Rehabilitation.

■ Federal Employment Services

The federal government is required by law to be a model employer in the personnel practices it uses. Accordingly, individuals with disabilities should consider the possibility that a career in the federal service may meet their needs. The federal government is committed by law to the following goals:

- Recruitment should try to achieve a work force made up of qualified people from all segments of society, and selection and promotion should be based solely on merit, after fair and open competition.

- All employees and applicants should be treated fairly, without discrimination, and with proper regard for their privacy and constitutional rights....

- Discrimination on the basis of race, color, religion, sex, national origin, age, handicapping condition, marital status, or political affiliation.... (is prohibited). (AN INTRODUCTION TO THE MERIT SYSTEMS PROTECTION BOARD, pp. 7-8)

Use the services of the Office of Personnel Management ("OPM") to locate federal jobs. The address of OPM in Washington, D.C. is set forth below. You may wish to contact the OPM office serving your locale.

> U.S. Office of Personnel Management
> 1900 E Street, N.W.
> Washington, D.C. 20415
> (202) 606-2700

Also consult with your local Department of Labor office.

■ Bulletin Boards and Placement Offices

Check bulletin boards or inquire of universities, colleges, schools and organizations with which you are affiliated to see if available jobs are posted.

■ Private Employment Agencies

Private employment agencies are best used by professionals or the technically skilled for whom an employer will pay the fee. Check the reputation and track record of the agency carefully and understand any agency contract thoroughly before signing. Be sure that you are not being charged for their services. You may also use agencies that place people in temporary jobs that may sharpen skills and possibly lead to a permanent job.

■ Radio and Television

Occasionally, ads for job openings are broadcast. Check local cable stations for their policies and practices. For example, public access channels may provide some information on county and local government job openings.

■ Trade and Professional Journals

Trade and professional journals often carry employment ads. You may want to subscribe to those related to your field or review them at the public library.

FINDING THE JOB

■ Personnel Offices

Companies must post their job openings on site. You can visit the personnel offices of companies in which you are interested to check listings of current openings.

■ Job Fairs

Job fairs bring together employers who are eager to recruit applicants for specific job openings with job seekers. Each participating employer has a booth or display with information about the company. Recruiters offer job seekers the opportunity to fill out applications and participate in brief interviews on the spot.

D. THE COVER LETTER

As important as a well-written resume is, you first need to get a prospective employer to read it. You grab his or her attention through a personal sales letter, typically referred to as a cover letter. The cover letter highlights key items in your resume and has two objectives: 1] to show how you meet every listed requirement the prospective employer is seeking, and 2] to emphasize what additional strengths you offer that are relevant to the job. The lead paragraph should be written to capture the reader's attention. Use the middle paragraph to present your qualifications for the job. The closing paragraph should request an interview and offer thanks for the employer's consideration. A sample letter is presented in Appendix D.

Make a copy of the letter for your records. Write the date in your calendar so that you may follow up at a suitable time. Time your letter to arrive midweek. (Monday is the heaviest mail day, and Friday is wrap-up day.)

E. THE APPLICATION

1. THE APPLICATION FORM

You often will be asked to complete an application form, even if you have submitted a resume or have been called in for an interview. Be prepared! Almost certainly, you will need the following information: Social Security number, driver's license number, work experience (dates, company names, and addresses, supervisor's names, etc.), school and training experience (dates and places), military record, references (with their permission), addresses, phone numbers, emergency contact (name. address, and phone number).

Federal, state, and local equal employment opportunity laws prevent employers from asking applicants for certain personal information they once could legally acquire. Nonetheless, some companies may still request this information. Generally, an employer **may** ask you questions to determine whether you can perform the essential functions of the job for which you are applying. He may also require that you show yourself to be in good health. However, an employer **may not** ask whether you have a disability and **may not** require you to take a physical until after he has offered you the job. If the questions seem unreasonable, you should consider whether to refuse to answer them.

There is an exception to this rule. If you require assistance **in the application process itself**, the prospective employer may legitimately ask you what assistance you require. For example, personnel interviews may severely disadvantage an individual with a hearing impairment unless an interpreter is provided. An individual with an auditory processing impairment may be similarly disadvantaged. An individual who has a substantial sight impairment may require assistance in the process of completing an application form. The application process may be similarly difficult for an individual with severe dyslexia. So, if you require reasonable accommodation in the application process, make arrangements ahead of time for the assistance you need. If you require reasonable accommodation at this stage, you should discuss your disability openly with an emphasis on what you can do, not what you can't do. You have no more reason to apologize for a disability than you do for your gender, race, place of birth, religion, or age.

2. Tips For Preparing Applications

An application may be the principal basis the employer uses to determine whether to call you for an interview. The tips set forth below are presented to help you to complete the application to your best advantage.

If possible, get more than one copy of the form you are to complete (or make a xerox). Fill out the additional copy as a "first draft".

Complete the application by typing or printing legibly (always use black ink). Try to complete all items on the application form. If a section does not apply to you, write "N/A" for "not applicable" in that section. Account for all significant time in your work history. Use positive phrasing to account for significant periods when you were not working.

Avoid saying "fired," "terminated", or "laid-off" if possible. Consider which of the following reasons best describes your reason for leaving: seeking career advancement, to take a better job, better pay and benefits, seeking a more challenging job, career change, family or personal illness, company restructuring or general cut-back.

Make certain the information in your application can be substantiated. Assemble letters of recommendation, certificates, awards, transcripts, etc. so that you may take them to interviews. You may attach your resume to the application to provide additional information regarding your work history, but do not substitute a resume for the work history section of the application. Finally, review the completed application and, of course, sign and date it.

F. TELEPHONING

Whether you are seeking a specific position or gathering preliminary information, the goal of every telephone contact you make is to get an interview. Think of all people to whom you talk not as obstacles but as gateways to help you reach your goal. Courtesy is not only appropriate but will also help achieve your goal. Write out the basic telephone presentation you will use. Practice until it becomes almost second nature. Anxiety will lessen with time and practice. Listen carefully to the responses you get and evaluate your approach periodically.

After you get to the right person, introduce yourself and identify the position you want, you are ready to "hook" the employer's interest. This can be the most important part of your telephone presentation. The hook is a concise statement outlining your skills, experience, and desires related to the position you are seeking.

Each person's hook will be different, so no universal sample will fit everyone. Here are two examples:

For a machinist:

"I can operate various drill presses, punch presses, latches and saws. I have an excellent performance record for accuracy during my two years as a machinist's helper."

For a beginner:

"I have basic laboratory skills that I learned in school, a strong academic record, and a real desire to excel in this area. I can begin at an entry level. I am willing to work hard and learn everything you can teach me."

Once you have thrown your hook, if you get a positive response from the employer, seek to set up an interview date. Otherwise, ask if the employer has time for an information interview. Such an interview is a preliminary technique to help you find out about kinds of jobs and particular companies. You may get leads as to other job possibilities.

G. SUMMARY

This Chapter provides strategies for getting organized, preparing a resume, finding job leads (in the hidden and visible job markets), preparing a cover letter and telephoning. Using one or more of these strategies should greatly increase the chances for success. As in everything else, polite persistence will eventually bring success.

5.

GETTING THE JOB

**Electronic Industries Foundation
Project With Industry Program**

A. INTRODUCTION

Now you've found the job for you. This Chapter concerns the next question: how do you get that job?

B. THE JOB INTERVIEW

Your application form was in order, your cover letter was compelling, your resume identified skills that meet the employer's needs, and now you've been asked to come in for a job interview. Prepare for the interview. Interviews allow employers to determine your willingness to do the job, your communication skills, your level of enthusiasm, and your "fit" into the organizational "family." Interviews are your opportunity to size up your potential employer. Is it a "family" you want to join?

■ What to Expect

There are two basic types of questions interviewers ask: **open- and closed-ended questions**. Open-ended questions require a complete, detailed response. Close ended questions can be answered by a single brief statement, a simple yes or no, or a date or place. Most interview questions will be open-ended. This allows employers to **gain** more information and to observe how you express yourself.

Employers form a profile of you during the interview based not only on your answers to the questions but also on how you answer them. They will consider your personality and your general achievements as well as your professional qualifications. Personal qualities might include: drive, motivation, communication skills, energy, determination, confidence, reliability, honesty, pride, dedication, analytical skills, and listening skills.

Think about what the employer wants and needs as you answer questions about yourself and your ability to do the job. Emphasize your abilities that are relevant to the job.

To help you prepare, Appendix E presents questions commonly asked at interviews. Take time to say, write or tape record answers to the questions. You may practice before a mirror. If you have access to a videocamera, it can be helpful to tape yourself and review the tape to correct flaws in your presentation. Finally, get a good night's sleep the night before the interview so that you will look your best and be alert.

■ Dressing for the Interview

Your appearance can greatly influence the employer's first impression of you. Select clothing that will create an image of professionalism and seriousness. Even if you will wear casual attire or a uniform on the job, dressing professionally for a job interview shows you understand that the interview is an important business occasion and suggests that you will represent the company well. Your overall appearance should project personable professionalism.

■ Interviewing Tips

Be early for the interview. Plan to be 15 minutes early.

Visit the restroom before you visit the employment office.

Smile at the outset and make frequent eye contact during the interview. Avoid looking at your watch or otherwise appearing distracted.

Use the interviewer's name a few times during the interview.

Speak clearly and precisely. Answer questions thoroughly but succinctly. Avoid one word answers. Remember the recruiter is trying to get to know you.

Let the interviewer set the pace of the interview and decide when to bring it to a conclusion. Listen carefully. Avoid interrupting the interviewer. If you are asked if you have any questions, go ahead and ask any questions you may have so that you will leave the interview with a thorough understanding of the job under discussion.

■ Following up on the Interview

Follow up after the interview by sending a thank you letter. It gives you a second opportunity to sell yourself and emphasize your ability to do the job. Appendix F presents a sample follow-up thank you letter.

C. EMPLOYMENT TESTS

Many employers give tests to ascertain the skill levels of applicants. Find out if a test is involved before going to an interview. This is especially important if you will need assistance with the testing procedure. Let the employer know beforehand what accommodations you will need, such as an untimed test. If possible, obtain a sample test and practice in advance. If you conclude that you do not have the ability to take the test, be honest with the employer and see if you can obtain a waiver.

Arrive early enough to get a comfortable seat with little distraction, perhaps in the front or a corner of the room. Have two of your own pencils available. Be sure lighting and space is adequate for your needs. Read the directions carefully. Ask questions about any directions that are unclear.

Read the questions carefully. Answer the easy questions first, then go back to the more difficult questions within each section. If you have to guess, go with your first impression; do not change your answer. Research has found that your first guess is usually correct. Some individuals with specific learning disabilities and attention deficit disorder see greater complexities in the questions than were intended by the test-giver. Going with your first impression may counteract this tendency. On the other hand, some individuals with these impairments read too rapidly, picking out a word or two on which they focus, while mentally "filling in the blanks" for the words they skipped over.

Double check dates if they are part of the question or answer. Dates are among the most easily scrambled items in a question or answer. In multiple choice formats, eliminate the items that are most obviously incorrect, then select the response that best answers the question.

If you have time, read the questions again and check your answers for any mistakes or errors. In timed situations, do not keep watching the clock. It takes valuable time that would be better used in taking the test!

D. THE JOB OFFER

When the offer has been made, you have a decision to make. You can accept the offer or decline it. Think carefully about the aspects of work that are most important to you and base your decision upon how well the job meets your criteria. Important facets to think about include salary, location, opportunities for promotion, opportunities to learn as well as to contribute, future co-workers, benefits, and shift (hours and times you will be working).

1. QUESTIONS TO ASK

■ Ask Yourself

As you weigh your decision, ask yourself the following questions:

Are the salary, benefits and hours acceptable? If they are not, are my expectations reasonable and do they reflect the current job market?

Am I able to arrive at work on time using the transportation available to me? If the job site is far from home, will I be able to abide the long daily commute? (If not, you may begin arriving late and/or become dissatisfied with the job.)

Am I considering this job because I really want it or because nothing else is available? (If you accept a job only for the steady paycheck "until something better comes along," your lack of enthusiasm will reflect in your job performance. If you do leave quickly for a better job, your job history may suggest you are a job hopper and an undependable employee.)

Does the job advance my long-term goals? (Remember goals should be reviewed and updated every five years. They may change dramatically over your lifetime.)

■ Ask the Employer

A job offer is your opportunity to ask additional questions about the job and about the company. Use it. Here are some sample questions:

Can I expect always to work the same shift I have been hired to work or are there rotations?

Are there regularly scheduled performance evaluations with clearly defined criteria?

How often are raises given and when might the first one be expected? What are the potentials for promotion and does the job lead into management positions?

By asking questions beforehand, you will minimize disappointments if you accept the job or missed opportunities if you decline.

Consider all facets of the job in your decision making. If only one aspect of the job ranks lower than you would like (the salary, for example), but the others score high by your standards, you are in luck. No job will meet all your expectations. The wise job seeker accepts an otherwise excellent opportunity when only one facet falls short.

2. DECLINING THE JOB OFFER

If you decide to decline a job offer, you should let the employer know immediately by phone or in person. Follow up with a letter thanking the employer, saying something positive about the position and giving a concrete reason for turning the offer down.

EXAMPLE: Although I am impressed with the mission of the company and eager to work in the area this job entails, after much thought I have decided I must decline your offer. I am convinced that I am ready for a management-track position. Should one open up with your firm, I would like to resubmit an application and hope you will consider my qualifications again at that time.

The courtesy of a prompt and polite refusal will count in your favor should the employer have another job in the future or know of an opening elsewhere.

3. ACCEPTING THE JOB OFFER

As soon as you decide to accept a job, let the employer know in person or by phone. At that time, discuss the following issues:

- Any disability you have decided to disclose at that time.

- Your understanding of accommodations the employer has agreed to make or provide.

- When your first day of work will be.

- What you need to bring with you (e.g., uniform, information).

- Where and to whom you should report on your first day of work.

■ Final salary and benefit negotiations.

After this conversation, send the employer a letter that confirms your acceptance of the job and your understanding of what was discussed during the conversation. Express thanks for the confidence shown in hiring you. Request that the employer send you written confirmation of your employment.

4. Leaving the Current Position

When the time comes for you to leave a job that has been a disappointment, follow these techniques to protect your future, maintain your dignity, and show some class.

■ Keep your search discreet.

■ Avoid bad-mouthing your current situation. As soon as you have the opportunity to leave and, only rarely before, notify your supervisor that you are leaving.

■ Learn the appropriate procedures for leaving and follow them. For example, some companies ask for two weeks' notice, others for three or more, especially for management level staff. Verify whether a resignation letter is appropriate. Find out what will happen to unused annual or sick leave, whether medical benefits terminate on the last day of employment, and whether you can extend them at your expense, if necessary.

■ When you have been unhappy, letters of resignation may tempt you to "tell it like it is." Resist the urge. Save your complaints for the exit interview. Your written resignation is a permanent record that will be in your file long after your anger or discontent has been resolved. Your letter should be positive and brief.

■ Resignation letters are unnecessary if you have been fired or laid off. If you have a grievance, follow the appropriate procedures; maintain a professional demeanor, keeping rein on you emotions. Get legal and psychological help if you need it. While you serve out your notice period, maintain a high level of productivity. After you have left, refrain from speaking against the company or divulging its secrets.

E. DISCLOSURE OF A DISABILITY

1. Talking About the Disability

You must consider disclosure of your disability at three points: 1] if you require reasonable accommodations in job testing 2] if you will require reasonable accommodations to perform the essential functions of the job and 3] if you believe that reasonable accommodations may be necessary in order for you to be promoted. Disclosure may also be necessary, as a practical matter, if your disability is obvious on meeting you or in reviewing your record. Otherwise, the decision as to whether and when to disclose is up to you. Your legal rights are discussed in Chapter 9.

2. Whether to Discuss the Disability with Employers

You are under no obligation to disclose your disability unless you require reasonable accommodations. However, you must weigh the outcomes of disclosure versus nondisclosure and come to your own personal decision. Employers may be influenced subconsciously and directly by a variety of factors. Disclosure may increase the likelihood that you might be placed in a dead-end job or that the employer may look for reasons to dismiss you later. Moreover, even if you identify your disability, you may still be faced with a lack of understanding as to precisely what reasonable accommodations should be provided in your case. The needs of an individual with a physical impairment are reasonably easy to assess. Attention deficit disorder and specific learning disabilities are usually not obvious at the outset, and the specific symptoms vary substantially from one individual to another. Moreover, they often pose problems that will become obvious, such as lateness, disorganization, and grammatical and spelling errors in written work. Additionally, there is often a lack of understanding of these disabilities and how they affect performance in the workplace. That lack of understanding exists in a broad range of individuals, including some who are well educated and well meaning. There are even some medical and educational professionals who are not well informed concerning these particular disabilities. Be aware that your employer may not be sufficiently conversant with the nature of your disability to discuss reasonable accommodations easily. You may have to provide specific information about your disability and your needs.

Consider the impact of keeping your disability a secret. Nondisclosure can create enormous stress. You have no way of knowing what level of support the company or your co-workers would give you. Your employer can not prepare in advance to accommodate you if he does not know you have a disability. Finally, if you choose not to disclose your disability and you build a record of what appears to be lateness, disorganization, and sloppy work, you may be put in the position of requesting reasonable accommodation for the first time when your job is in jeopardy. Raising the matter at that time may cause your request to lack credibility in the eyes of your employer and further complicate the process of reasonable accommodation.

The bottom line for many individuals is this: if you believe that you have a reasonable prospect of performing the job (including compliance with rules regarding lateness, deadlines, etc.) without a reasonable accommodation, it may not be necessary to disclose the disability. If, on the other hand, it is your judgement that your job performance will not be perceived as adequate unless there is a reasonable accommodation, then disclosure is probably necessary.

There is a middle ground between full formal disclosure and no disclosure. It won't work for everyone, but it might be worth considering. If you have an auditory processing problem, for example, it might be worth raising informally with your supervisor the problem you are experiencing on the job. Let him know that you will need to double-check your instructions to make sure that you have them correct. If you are late to work, describe the difficulty and reassure the employer that you are more than happy to make up the missed work that day. By using informal techniques such as this, you increase the chances that your employer will be motivated to extend practical accommodations to you. Moreover, he will be more likely to view you as having a "problem" that you are conscientiously working on, rather than a poor attitude towards your work.

If you decide to disclose your disability, learn to be honest and comfortable discussing it. Think of it as another of your characteristics to be discussed, like your education and your work history. Understand that employers may have concerns about your disability. Try to anticipate this and provide positive reassurance.

What accommodations may facilitate your proficiency and what do they cost? The good news about attention deficit disorder and specific learning disabilities is that the accommodations which are most successful are also relatively inexpensive.

Employers may raise these and other, similar legitimate concerns during the discussions. To sell yourself as a strong candidate, be confident, knowledgeable, and prepared to answer. One valuable free resource for information about accommodations is the Job Accommodation Network (1-800-526-7234). Operators can tell you about all the different types of accommodations and the costs of each.

As you discuss your disability, keep your explanation brief. Use lay language; medical terminology tends to frighten people. Be nonchalant and matter-of-fact. Your obvious acceptance of your condition will help others to accept it, too. Whatever you do, don't become defensive. Make your discussion job related. Move as quickly as possible from a brief description to a discussion of what you can do. Remember, that the focus of this interview is your qualifications for the job.

Practice will increase your comfort level. Review and rehearse what you want to say with family members, friends and advisors. If you convey a sense of comfort, the employer is more likely to be comfortable as well.

3. WHEN TO DISCUSS THE DISABILITY

If you decide to disclose a hidden disability, generally, you may wish to do so at the time you are offered a job. This is not deceitful. You are keeping the selection process focused on your skills and abilities--on what you can do--until the employer has decided that the company can use your unique blend of skills, experience and personality to meet its objectives. The negotiation period between job offer and acceptance is the time when you and the employer discuss salary, benefits, hours, and other potentially variable aspects of the job. It may be appropriate at this time to disclose your disability and any accommodations that might be necessary or helpful to you in performing the essential functions of the position.

Knowing the law, being prepared to discuss your disability, and knowing when to initiate the discussion will make it easier to talk openly with the employer about your disability, accommodations, and how you can successfully perform the job.

F. SUMMARY

Getting the job may involve [1] preparing for, attending and following up on the job interview, [2] taking the employment test, [3] considering and deciding whether to accept the job offer and [4] considering disclosure of a disability.

6.

ON THE JOB

Dale S. Brown
Peter S. Latham, J.D.

A. INTRODUCTION

You've passed the test! Now you have a job. When that happens, the focus of your life will change. You are no longer faced with the problems of finding a job. Now you are faced with the questions 1] how can I advance in my chosen career and 2] how can I prevent or minimize problems in the workplace which might cost me the job I worked so hard to get? These are issues for every person in the workforce and every individual with disabilities, but they are particularly challenging for an individual with attention deficit disorder or a specific learning disability, since these impairments often present problems in social adaptability, as well as in doing certain job tasks, and thus make the workplace that much more challenging.

This Chapter is divided into two parts: getting ahead while on the job and how to handle trouble when it starts.

B. GETTING AHEAD

1. ADVANCEMENT ISSUES

Job advancement is challenging for everyone but the challenge is particularly difficult for people with disabilities. In the 1990s, a glut of managers, the movement of "baby boomers" into mid-level positions, and corporate downsizing have increased the difficulty of moving up in traditional organizations. It is wise to start thinking about promotion potential when you interview for or accept the job.

During the discussion, find a way to mention your interest in the future. You may want to ask, "Where does this job lead?" and "What happened to the person who held this position?"

If it is a generic position within the company, ask, "What jobs do the people in this position do after five years?" This shows the employer that you intend to stay with the company and may break the stereotype that a person with a disability wants to stay in the same job forever.

Assess your future boss. If he or she appears to be moving up, you may move up with your manager. Ask them how they got to where they are today.

When discussing reasonable accommodation, make every effort to keep all of the responsibilities that are part of the job, particularly those that will help you advance.

For example, a manager may hire a person with a learning disability and remove team management elements from the position, because he or she believes a person with this disability has social skills deficits. Supervision and leadership lead to advancement. For this reason, if you have disclosed your disability, ask the manager to describe the accommodations the firm will provide and assure that they will not hamper your advancement in the future.

2. BE AN EXCELLENT EMPLOYEE

Once you are hired, you need to be an excellent employee. Most successful people with disabilities report that they are treated in a manner similar to that of other minorities. It is necessary for them to be significantly better than their peers in order to keep their jobs. Advancement, however, requires more than doing a good job.

Volunteer to perform work that expands your responsibilities. If something needs to be done that is a higher level than your present job, do it even if it takes extra time. Network within the company to become aware of needs and openings as they arise. Be sure that your boss and top management are aware of your activities. This can be achieved through discussions and memos.

Remember, appearing to do a good job is as important as actually doing a good job. The impression that you are making is as important as what you are actually doing.

Unfortunately, disabilities can get in the way of your supervisor seeing you for what you are. Therefore, you may need to make some extra effort to have your competence recognized.

Conversely, others may have such low expectations, that everything you do well is considered "amazing." You will need to do everything possible to counteract this prejudice.

One way to develop a positive image is to gain visibility outside the company. Consider joining a professional association, networking with colleagues, volunteering for projects, writing articles and running for office within an organization.

Richard Pimentel, senior vice president, Winmills Training Group, who has trained thousands of employers regarding the hiring and recruiting of people with disabilities, points out that supervisors are often hesitant to give feedback to people with disabilities.

"Suppose two employees are painting widgets," he suggests. "Instead of painting them red, they paint them yellow. Now, Mary is non-disabled and Tom is blind. So, the boss goes to Mary and says, 'Hey, Mary, you're painting the widgets the wrong color! Paint them red. RED. You got that?'

"But, why is Tom painting the widgets yellow? Because he's disabled. The boss is afraid to tell Tom to paint the widgets red. So, he tells everyone else how incompetent Tom is and that disabled people won't work out."

To counteract this problem, Pimentel says that people with disabilities need to request effective reality checks. "Make an appointment with your boss," he advises. "Ask him or her how you are doing. Ask, "How is my production? How can I improve? How can I get along better with you?" Listen to the response and act on the advice.

After a year or more on the job, Pimentel recommends making a plan with your supervisor for promotion. He suggests that you say, "I'm interested in a promotion. What is your understanding of what's possible? What do I need to do? Can you introduce me to people?"

You and your supervisor can modify your job to give you the experience you need for promotion. You will have to ask your supervisor about the promotion, perhaps because someone told them when you were hired that you would stay where you are. You can be promoted, but it's a lot of work.

3. Up the Ladder

Here are some things you can do at the entry level which can help with promotion.

■ **Cultivate a positive self-image.** Many people with disabilities feel "grateful to have a job." Remember that your employer should be happy to have you on the job.

■ **Avoid unrealistic expectations.** Some people with disabilities have experienced unrealistic positive feedback throughout childhood in the special education system. Unrealistic expectations can not be sustained in most jobs. Getting a job is exciting. But some people with disabilities (particularly attention deficit disorder) may have a tendency to entertain unrealistic expectations. A security guard may see himself as doing the work of "Dirty Harry." A paralegal may see herself as a Supreme Court Justice in the making. Unrealistic expectations of these types frequently lead to arrogance and a feeling that the job is a dead end, when a more balanced perspective would lead to the conclusion that the work is interesting and rewarding in itself.

■ **Avoid arrogance.** Unrealistic expectations can lead to a poor attitude in another way. Some individuals with learning disabilities and attention deficit disorder accept jobs alongside people with lesser educational backgrounds. If you feel that you are better than others on your job or that your job is below you, you should 1] remind yourself that all work is valuable and 2] monitor your behavior so that any initial negative feelings you may have do not show.

■ **Your manager is not your parent.** Remember that managers are managers, not parents or teachers. They are willing to be helpful but do not have any responsibility for your personal life. They will not necessarily compliment you for a job well done. They frequently have limited time to teach you.

■ **Extra hours can help you advance.** Extra hours can help you advance, if you spend the extra time fulfilling duties that are at a higher level than your current job. Many successful individuals with learning disabilities and/or attention deficit disorder report that long hours were a common experience for them.

■ **Your advancement is important.** Your work towards a promotion helps all employees with learning disabilities and attention deficit disorder.

■ **You are engaged in a learning process.** The learning process you engage in while working towards a promotion is as important as receiving the promotion. Keeping this in mind enables you to relax about seeking a promotion. People who have spent their childhoods under strong stress often become overly determined and undermine their own progress.

■ **The challenge of success.** People with disabilities have a particularly difficult time receiving promotions. However, through choosing a job with the potential for advancement, assuring that reasonable accommodation does not remove challenges, working hard, being visible, communicating well with the supervisor and others on the job, and developing self-confidence, it is still possible to climb the ladder of success.

■ **Select a positive role model.** As you move up, the techniques of success change. It is essential to study the expected behaviors of the top people and emulate them. Some of the above advice will always be helpful, but other parts may change.

■ **Don't forget self-employment.** Some individuals (with or without disabilities and with or without accommodations) are not most highly productive working for other people. If advancement is denied you, and you have fairly considered the strategies suggested in this book, plus others you have developed for yourself, it may be that self-employment is the key to success. If you reach this conclusion, the 1990s appear to have been made for you. The revolution in computer technology, coupled with desk-top publishing, fax machines and modems has made possible an entirely new approach to working. Many people operate successful and profitable service businesses from their homes. Clerical assistance is often provided by others who work out of **their** homes and are are linked by telephone, fax machine and modem. The day of the rugged individualist has been re-invented!

C. IF THERE'S TROUBLE

This is a book about success in the work place, and so it seems almost out of place to talk about trouble - what might go wrong. But the hard fact is that at some time or other virtually every individual, with or without a disability, will experience a set-back in his or her career, whether it is a failure to obtain a desired promotion, a demotion, lay-off, or termination. How you handle a set-back can be more important than how you handle success.

This Chapter can be particularly important for individuals with learning disabilities and attention deficit disorder, because those disabilities are often accompanied by deficits in socialization which make job trouble harder to foresee, more startling when it occurs, and more challenging to the individual's self-esteem than it would be for others who do not have these disabilities.

One story will serve as an example. PB was a writer for a newspaper in a major city. His writing skills were excellent, but he also was an individual with attention deficit disorder. As a result of his impairment, he frequently forgot the security pass he was required to display when entering his firm's building on the weekends. There were a number of complaints about his failure to display the pass. Matters came to a head one weekend. Confronted with an important deadline, PB rushed to work, again forgetting his pass. He was absorbed in the process of mentally composing his story as he rushed through the lobby of his building and "blew past" the security desk without, of course, displaying his pass. The guard, whom PB knew by sight (and who knew PB by sight) refused to allow him entry. Startled, PB said: "You know who I am, and I'm in a hurry - I've got a deadline." When the guard continued to refuse, PB insulted him, boarded the elevator and went to his office to work on his story. The guard, by this time furious at PB's insults, called his superiors who contacted PB's employer. The employer, confronted with repeated prior security breaches, and a (by now) inflammatory incident, fired PB on the spot. Outraged, PB explained: "But I was only doing my job!." In PB's mind, the security incidents were like so many speeding tickets - unfortunate, but unrelated to his work. To the employer, they were breaches of company rules which required that employees - in addition to performing their functions- must also be "good citizens" - i.e. punctual, courteous, and orderly in their workplace behavior.

This case need never have happened. If PB had taken a broader view of his duties, and considered compliance with security procedures as part of his job, he would have been as conscientious about carrying his pass and cooperating with the security procedures as he was about his deadlines. If PB had had the benefits of Dr. Nadeau's advice on strategies (see Chapter 3), he might well have adopted a means of ensuring that he complied with the rules. Further, he might have obtained as an accommodation, the employer's agreement that he undertake his weekend work at home or that he have a special arrangement with security personnel - the right to obtain a temporary visitor's security pass for gaining entry to the building in place of returning to his home to get his regularly issued pass, for example.

This is not a chapter about legal rights - that's Chapter 9. This one is about **damage control** - what you should do to avoid trouble or to minimize trouble once it erupts. If PB had politely gone home to get his pass, he might have been chewed out for being late and he might even have endangered his deadline, but the odds are that he would not have been fired. His employer would still have the services of a top-notch writer; he would still be employed by that newspaper.

This portion of the Chapter is based on the optimistic premise that individuals (both employers and employees) acting in good faith can solve most problems through honest and open discussion. That premise is not universally a valid one. Not every employee has the self-knowledge, self-discipline and drive to handle serious strains on the working relationship. Not every employer will have the insight, compassion and commitment to individuals with disabilities to make a potentially difficult situation better. As a result, many employment relationships go beyond the point of no return before they can be salvaged. When that happens, the employee has little choice but to rethink his or her job strategies, re-evaluate his strengths and weaknesses, locate another job, or (in appropriate cases) assert his or her legal rights. However, not all problems need to become insoluble. Here are some thoughts on strategies that might prove helpful.

1. SOCIAL REQUIREMENTS OF JOBS

Most people, when they think of job "requirements" consider only the academic qualifications, required on-the-job experience, and competence in the work itself required of the employee. However, this book is being written because, a job has more requirements - ones that "go without saying" to most of us. The "silent requirements" of jobs include 1] cooperativeness in the work situation, both with fellow employees and supervisors 2] compliance with "good citizenship" rules, e.g. being on time; no unauthorized absences; no smoking, etc. and 3] a record of "off the job conduct" which is reasonably free from convictions for offenses whose commission may affect job performance. Moreover, these "silent requirements" become increasingly important as the seniority and pay of the positions increase.

2. SIGNS OF TROUBLE

There's an excellent cartoon about a trial you should consider. The Judge has turned to the jury and has asked whether the jury has reached a verdict. The jury Foreman (who is tying a hangman's knot) replies that it has. The humor lies in the fact that the Foreman's answer is unnecessary. He has made it clear through his conduct that 1] a decision has been reached and 2] it is a guilty verdict.

Some signs of trouble in the workplace are almost as obvious. Others are subtle. Here are some of them.

■ Negative Comments From Co-Workers and Supervisors

Trouble can begin with negative comments from co-workers and supervisors. Snide or sarcastic comments about lateness, disorganization or sloppiness in your work can be evidence of a growing perception that your job performance is not "up to the company's standards." If you do not understand a comment, write it down. For example, one boss said to an employee with learning disabilities, "Finally, you made it here on time. I'm glad to see you." The employee was lucky. A co-worker explained, "He's trying to tell you not to be late again." If these perceptions have any basis in fact, and the comments are repeated, it may be time for you to meet with your supervisor and request an informal review of your job performance to date. This technique can defuse a situation before it becomes ugly.

■ Informal "Chats" About "Good Citizenship"

Frequently, a decision to withhold pay increases, deny promotion or fire someone is arrived at over a period of time. When things are going wrong, sometimes, a supervisor will have a "chat" with an employee about the standards of performance required by the company. Frequently the supervisor is not comfortable with a direct statement such as, "You're frequently late, and I'm going to have to do something about it." Such confrontations may trigger responses such as, "Its not my fault. It's all the traffic I have to go through." As a result, a supervisor's first approach to the problem may be indirect, in the hopes that you will "get the hint." Discussions of this type might include statements like, "We here at X Corp. pride ourselves on being on time and ready for work." If you have such a conversation, don't assume that the supervisor is simply passing on information about company attitudes for no reason. He or she is either 1] correct in the perception that your lateness has been a problem or 2] incorrect. In either event, the supervisor's concerns should be addressed. It may be helpful to ask, "Do you feel I'm not meeting the standards? Could you tell me how I fall short?"

■ Less Desirable Assignments

Some supervisors, faced with a perception that an employee's performance is substandard, may react by assigning individuals to less desirable work, either in the hope that they will become dissatisfied with the job and leave, or in the belief that the desirable work (and the potential for advancement) should go to more deserving workers. If this happens, don't "blow your top." Perform the work required for a period of time to the extent necessary. Show your dedication to the company in as many ways as you can. Then ask to meet with your supervisor and explore the possibility of re-assignment after you have shown that the company's needs come first. However, less desirable assignments are often a sign that the job relationship has been irreparably damaged and so even these strategies may not work.

■ Extra Work and Weekend Work

Other supervisors, faced with a perception that an employee's performance is substandard, may react by assigning individuals to extra work and weekend work. The previous comments apply to this situation also. Do not argue that you have worked hard all week and are unwilling to accept the work.

■ Complaints About "Overly Rigid " Adherence to Rules

Some individuals with attention deficit disorder and learning disabilities work so hard at complying with the rules that they become overly invested in following them. Seeing other employees and management ignore these rules can be infuriating. It is *always* inappropriate to comment on anyone else's following or not following the rules. Your major job is monitoring your own behavior. Gauge the level of strictness with which your company rules are enforced. Watch what people do, not what the policy manuals say. Does everyone come in at the starting time? When do they usually leave? What about reports? One woman was the only person in her office who filled out meeting reports, which were technically required. She spent her time doing a job which was in fact unnecessary. Another individual, for example, endangered his job by leaving work at the precise moment his watch displayed the designated quitting time, regardless of what other activities were taking place. A supervisor, confronted with the departure of an employee at 5:00 P.M. in the middle of a conversation is unlikely to take a charitable view of the matter.

■ Transferring Your Work to Others

Sometimes a supervisor will transfer portions of an employee's work to others rather than face the prospect of correcting the employee if he perceives the confrontation will be uncomfortable, or if he perceives that he is not "getting through" to the employee. Again, a combination of initial willing acceptance, followed by an informal job evaluation review with the supervisor and a request for correction of the situation are the best remedies. However, work re-assignment is often a sign that the job relationship has been irreparably damaged and so even these strategies may not work. (It is sadly true that a few employers are willing to undertake far more extensive job restructuring efforts in order to eliminate an employee than to accommodate him.)

■ Negative Performance Evaluations

No one can miss the significance of a negative performance evaluation. These are best handled by an honest and direct discussion of your deficiencies and a request for guidance. Do not respond simply by arguing that "Everyone is late." or that "Ms. X has the same quality of work as I do, but you never complain about her." Agree that you understand the serious nature of the supervisor's concern (even if you disagree with it) and enlist him or her as a partner in correcting matters.

■ Promotion of Others with Less Seniority

Another sign can be the promotion of individuals with less seniority. If this is repeated, and you receive no promotion, it is again time for an informal performance review.

■ Arguments with Supervisors

Be careful when you disagree with your supervisor. If he or she is wrong, your task is education of the supervisor and correction of the situation through the techniques we have discussed. If the supervisor is right, you need to correct the situation and let the company know you are doing so, cheerfully. Above all else, do not begin to call in sick or refuse assignments as a means of avoiding working for someone who is distasteful to you. No one, with or without a disability has the right to refuse work or to refuse to work for a particular supervisor. Do not argue that other employees have engaged in conduct worse than that which your supervisor is discussing. It is like telling a police officer that he shouldn't give you a speeding ticket because another motorist was going even faster than you were. If, however, the work situation has truly become intolerable, turn to Chapter 4: Finding a Job.

3. OUTSIDE HELP

It is essential to gain perspective. Try to have some mentors outside of the job with whom you can discuss work events. After any event that bothers you, reflect on it and write it down. Note down who was present and what was actually said. Then remember non-verbal communication. Often, non-verbal communication creates a feeling which is different from the words actually used. Note your feelings about the meeting, even if they result in a picture of the meeting which is different from the words actually used.

Describe the meeting to your mentors and ask their opinions. Enlist all members of your social network who know about your disability and are supportive. The social side of work is a serious challenge for people with learning disabilities and attention deficit disorder. You deserve and should seek out a support team to provide coaching and advice. Ask your parents and friends. Stay in touch with college counselors and professors - they may be willing to advise you on occasion. Contact your local Learning Disabilities Association of America chapter and see if one of the members would be willing to mentor you. When you ask for help, ask for it in a time-limited way, e.g., "Would you be willing to meet with me for one hour a month/quarter and help me with work related issues?" Then prepare for the meeting and use the mentor's time well.

Cultivate relationships with co-workers and managers who are not your direct supervisor. Consider talking to co-workers about these difficulties and asking their assessment. People who leave your workplace are extremely valuable as mentors. They know the "cast of characters" and may be willing to talk freely with you.

4. Talking with the Supervisor

There is an art to talking with your supervisor. Here are a few points to bear in mind.

■ In asking your supervisor for feedback, be sensitive. Your supervisor may not be able to explain exactly what the problem is. He or she may may just have a strong negative feeling, without being able to articulate it. This is an extremely awkward situation for both of you, because the negative reactions may be due to your behavior or may be prejudice on the supervisor's part.

■ People with ADD/LD sometimes have visible signs of their central nervous system dysfunction which cause others to be uneasy in their presence. They may occur in discussions with your supervisor, co-workers and others. These signs may result from their need **consciously** to monitor their physical movements, an activity which others perform "without thinking." Active monitoring requires attention as does the social content of the meeting. Together, the active monitoring and the social tracking demands overload the individual's capacity for sustained attention. As a result, the individual with these disabilities either 1] loses part of the conversation or 2] loses track of his or her physical movements. Examples of such visible signs include: fidgeting, holding the head at an angle, staring, blinking too much, asymmetrical facial movements, moving in jerks rather than smoothly, sitting in a ramrod straight, "at attention" posture. It is worth tremendous effort and discipline to control these "soft neurological signs." Some individuals have found that videotaping a "rehearsal" of a meeting is helpful in this regard. Unfortunately, it may not be possible to control them, and prejudice may be the result. People may feel uneasy when they first meet you and not know why. You may be denied the benefit of the doubt. In this case, try not to internalize the negative non-verbal messages that you may receive on occasion.

■ Some strategies for the problem of a supervisor who has trouble explaining his negative feelings are as follows: 1] write a note to your supervisor asking for a meeting and give him time to reflect 2] after you have heard your supervisor out, ask for time to think about your response and check his/her feedback with others 3] make it easy for your supervisor to talk to you. Say, "Nobody's performance is perfect. What are things I can do to be excellent?"

■ If you have auditory/perceptual problems, you may need to request written guidance. This is an option if you tend to "blow up" when you are criticized verbally. Unfortunately, your supervisor may be afraid to point out anything in writing due to today's litigious climate. Also, in most organizations, written negative feedback is the start to disciplinary action. Some things to say are, "Would it be possible for you to jot down some notes informally about things I could do better? After I review it, we can throw it out." You might also say, "I need your guidance but its tough for me to hear it and may be tough for you to say it. Is there any possibility you can write down some ways I could do better?"

5. TERMINATION

Sometimes trouble cannot be avoided. If you are terminated from your employment, endure the ordeal with style. You may be remembered favorably for the grace with with you left the company. Remember, you may have to list this employment on a future job application form. If he is asked, an employer can say, "Yes, " X worked here, and we were sorry it didn't work out. She has many admirable skills, but the match wasn't quite right." The employer can also say, "Yes, X worked here, and we had to fire her. She was never on time, she was constantly disorganized and when she did deign to put in an appearance, her work was poor." Which would you prefer? Your conduct will decide which one is used. The name of the game (even in your final moments with the company) is **damage control**.

One final thought. If you have not disclosed your disability and you believe your difficulties with the job result from that disability, you may wish to consider identifying your disability and requesting reasonable accommodation. This is unlikely to prevent termination, but it is necessary if you intend to contest the decision to terminate your employment through a grievance procedure or litigation. It may also be useful in negotiating a face saving resignation as an alternative to termination, and it may limit the extent to which the employer will subsequently "bad-mouth" you.

D. SUMMARY

None of these strategies guarantees success. However, using one or more with which you are comfortable will greatly increase the chances for success. As in everything else, polite persistence will eventually bring success.

7.

PERSONAL STORIES

Patricia H. Latham, J.D.
Peter S. Latham, J.D.

A. INTRODUCTION

This chapter describes personal experiences of individuals with attention deficit disorder and learning disabilities in the workplace.

An example is Charles Schwab, the founder and chief executive officer of Charles Schwab & Co., a leading, national discount brokerage firm based in California. Though a highly successful financier and entrepreneur, he has struggled throughout his life with dyslexia - specifically, problems with reading and spelling. Nonetheless, he earned a degree in economics from Stanford University and later an MBA. Charles Schwab did more than succeed in **spite** of his dyslexia; he succeeded **because** of it. His insights into information processing in the brokerage business stemmed in part from his struggle with dyslexia.

Mr. Schwab's success was described in the June 1992 issue of FORTUNE, magazine: "Having struggled his entire life to process information, Schwab built his company to do precisely that for investors - process the information needed to make sound investment decisions". He seeks to "empower" his customers with information from many different sources so that investors may make informed decisions.

Not only has Charles Schwab brought his considerable talent, energy and drive to the brokerage business, but he and his wife Helen have established the Parent Education Resource Center in San Mateo, California. The Center provides services and counseling for parents of children with learning disabilities. His success in both overcoming the potential barrier of dyslexia and making this apparent impediment work for him, is inspirational.

Like Charles Schwab, a number of individuals with ADD and LD have achieved national recognition in science, engineering, architecture, business, the arts, the media and other fields. Many other individuals with ADD and LD have succeeded in various types of work within their communities. The personal experiences described below reflect continuing struggle and may be meaningful to a wide range of individuals with ADD and LD who are seeking to contribute talents and reap rewards in the workplace.

B. EXPERIENCES

All of the stories that follow are the result of interviews conducted by the editors in preparing this book. The stories demonstrate that there are many paths to success. While each person's story merits a book in itself, we have summarized their stories and emphasized those aspects of them which are relevant to this text. Their life experiences are both moving and heroic: moving because of the pain which many of these individuals felt as they struggled; heroic because they and their families at times struggled alone and without the kinds of support and information that are now becoming available. The stories have one thing in common, however. **The individuals never gave up.** They have found their way in the workplace and tailored it to fit their personal strengths and disabilities. Some have fulfilled their expectations. Others are continuing toward that goal. In doing so, they have confirmed that specific learning disabilities and attention deficit disorder can be viewed as a life style and not a life sentence. Their stories should serve to encourage others to persevere in their efforts to succeed in the workplace.

JAY

Jay is a college graduate in his twenties with attention deficit disorder and learning disabilities. He grew up knowing that he had ADD and LD and was in special education classes during his early years in school. Math classes were a nightmare. He also had problems with writing papers. His impulsivity and lagging social skills caused him problems with his peers. As Jay matured, his outgoing nature, good verbal skills and family support helped him emerge as a young adult able to accept himself and move toward achieving his goals.

Jay knew that he needed a job with no mathematics requirement, so he ruled out sales. He felt that police work would be interesting. He started as a security guard and then joined a local police force. He decided not to request accommodations on the job or in entrance testing. He had to carefully select which police force to join because some entrance tests had a mathematics section.

Once through the training and on the job, Jay was excited about his work and proud of his position. Driving patrol cars, moving around, sirens, bright lights and constant action made him feel eager about his duties and left him with a feeling of satisfaction at the end of his shift. Jay was comfortable with his peers and supervisors because the expectations were very clear. For the first time, he was even able to excel in courses because the work excited him.

He was promoted to detective. At first, he hesitated because he felt he would miss the excitement of the patrols. Still, he moved forward and found that he enjoyed the challenges of detective work.

There are aspects of his job that are not highly enjoyable for him, such as the paper work. However, his overall enjoyment of the job makes him able to focus on the paper work and get it done. He has not found it necessary to request accommodations.

ROBERT

Robert is in his mid-thirties. He was first diagnosed as having learning disabilities while in medical school, and is now in his final year.

Robert had completed college in his early twenties and had then worked successfully in state government for over ten years. He had felt during his school years that he was a bright person, but he did notice that he did not learn as quickly as many others. As he put it "it just takes me longer." Still, Robert wanted more than anything to be a doctor. After several tries on the medical school admission test, Robert was accepted to medical school. The first year of medical school was overwhelming for him. What had always seemed a minor difference in him suddenly seemed to be a major problem threatening to destroy his hopes for a medical career. He went for testing to determine if there might be a learning problem. Robert was diagnosed as having learning disabilities, specifically in the areas of auditory processing and short-term memory. Still, Robert felt that he could succeed, because he always had done so in the past. He was not comfortable with the idea of having a disability.

With little in the way of accommodations, Robert struggled painfully in medical school and finally reached the fourth year, only to find that he had failed an important course and was being dismissed from the school.

Having put in so much work to reach this point, Robert was determined to continue in medical school. He consulted with a number of professionals specializing in learning disabilities. He had psychoeducational testing, sought counseling with respect to strategies and accommodations and obtained legal advice. Then, Robert transferred to a medical school with support services for students with learning disabilities. With increased accommodations and support services, his own greater understanding of his learning disabilities and acceptance and belief in himself, Robert is now in the process of completing medical school.

KIM

Kim is in her thirties and balances working with her roles as wife and mother. She learned that she had attention deficit disorder only after her child was diagnosed as having the condition. Kim has known for some time that her strengths were in dealing with the public and in problem solving, part of her duties as a systems analyst. Likewise, she was aware of weaknesses, especially in performing tedious and repetitious tasks involved in computer programming.

Over the past several years, her job came to emphasize long term programming projects. She began to do less well and to feel very stressed. Just as Kim was learning that she had ADD, she got a bad review from her supervisor. The supervisor made it clear that Kim might be fired.

Kim informed her supervisor of the disability and requested accommodations recommended by her psychologist. Kim requested breaking the project into smaller segments with deadlines, clarification of instructions in writing and frequent feedback on her work through review meetings. At first, the supervisor seemed willing but then seemed to have difficulty doing the work to provide the accommodations. As a result, Kim came to realize that neither the job nor the supervisor was a good match for her. Kim decided to explore transferring to another position within the company, but soon found that there were no openings.

Kim began to look for another job that would be a better match. A few weeks into this process, Kim was fired. She decided to focus on her job search and not on trying to take action against her former employer.

She parted on good terms and was able to find a systems analyst job that was a good match for her. She knows what she needs from her employer and is seeking to get clear instructions and frequent feedback without disclosing that she has ADD. She is educating herself about ADD and has continued working with her psychologist on coping skills. She is now on medication and finds this helpful as well. Kim feels more relaxed and better about herself. After she has established a positive relationship with her employer, she will identify herself as ADD if she feels it is necessary.

JESSE

Jesse had recently been promoted to supervisor in a large manufacturing plant. After learning that his son had attention deficit disorder and encountering problems on the job, Jesse became aware that he had many of the traits that were causing problems for his son. Jesse went for an evaluation and was diagnosed as having ADD.

Jesse had to do a lot of organizing and tracking of materials and employee progress on projects. He felt that he was not coping well. It was easy for him to miss something. Soon he was receiving warnings about his performance.

Jesse scheduled a meeting with his supervisor to discuss ADD and the problems it was causing him on the job. At Jesse's suggestion, his doctor and supervisor met to discuss the problems. At Jesse's next meeting with his supervisor, they were able to arrange a transfer to another visible and responsible position in the plant that would be a better match for Jesse. He is now doing well on the job and feels especially pleased to be enjoying his work.

ALAN

Alan is a lawyer in his twenties. He was diagnosed as having learning disabilities after completing law school and encountering problems in the workplace.

Alan worked very hard to prepare for the Law School Admission Test and did quite well on the test and in law school. He attended a law school that had a practical and experiential approach to learning law. He did well on the bar exam.

Alan's greatest problems developed in the workplace. He has had difficulty getting and keeping a position as an attorney. He enjoyed analyzing legal issues but found the fast pace and high pressure of law offices stressful and almost paralyzing at times. After realizing that he was having difficulties, he had extensive neuropsychological testing which identified a number of specific learning disabilities. He then sought advice from the neuropsychologist and is developing an understanding of strategies he may use, and accommodations he may need.

At present Alan is self employed. He takes research assignments from a number of companies and agencies. He also teaches at a university and does volunteer legal work. This works well for him in some ways - setting his own pace and working independently, but he would like greater income and security.

CAROL

Carol is in her twenties and was diagnosed with moderate learning disabilities in early childhood. She had significant problems with auditory and visual processing, language and short-term memory. From the outset, her parents were very supportive and sought out information and opportunities.

Carol's entire education was in self-contained special education classes. She completed high school and then attended a two-year certificate program at a university. For Carol, learning in virtually every area, including social skills, is a slow and difficult process. With great effort, she has done well enough to live independently and work.

She tried several temporary jobs and then secured a clerical job at a federal agency. She enjoys having her own apartment and being near her family. Her goal is to continue with the agency and get a promotion.

DOUGLAS

Douglas is a college graduate in his late thirties who was recently diagnosed as having attention deficit disorder.

Douglas took extra time to complete college, dropping out briefly due to "burn out". Toward the end of college he married. Over the years, Douglas has held numerous jobs in the sales area, including, insurance broker and stock broker. Douglas enjoys the challenge of selling to people and explaining the product. He has difficulty with the follow up - especially the paper work - and becomes frustrated. At one point he felt "burnt out" and worked as a truck driver. He liked seeing new things and constantly being on the go. He felt freed of the responsibilities of planning, following up, etc., that had been so important in his prior jobs. He got some of the same feeling that his favorite hobbies (surfing and motorcycle riding) had given him - scenery seeming to rush toward him, sensory excitement and movement. Soon, however, in order to spend more time with his family, he returned to sales.

Douglas is now director of sales for a small technical company. Having been diagnosed as ADD, he is taking medication and finds that it helps him focus. In reflecting on his past, he feels that ADD caused him to feel easily bored and move frequently from job to job and place to place. He sees the need for support staff for the follow up tasks that are so difficult for him. Should he need to make job changes in the future, he feels better equipped to make suitable selections.

ALMA

Alma is in her early thirties, has attention deficit disorder and seems to thrive on constantly having a variety of tasks to ward off boredom.

She takes courses periodically and has completed several years of college. Her energy enables her to wear many hats - wife, mother, part time employee, entrepreneur and student. She works as a temp for a company that provides temporary office assistance. She enjoys the variety and finds it stimulating to meet new people each week and to use a wide range of computer equipment and programs. She also works part time as a music director and has started a small bookkeeping business.

Alma wishes to complete college and decide on a career direction. In the meantime, the mix she has put together works well for her.

VINCENT

Vincent is in his early twenties and has been struggling with his attention disorder symptoms since childhood.

Vincent attended a special education school and graduated at eighteen. He took stimulant medication during high school but then stopped, believing that he had outgrown ADD. After moving from job to job without finding anything that pleased him, Vincent decided to join the army for technical training. At basic training, Vincent did the required training but he could not handle what he perceived as harassment by his superiors. In the end, to his great disappointment, he was not able to complete basic training and received a discharge.

He has regrouped, moved forward and now is working as an assistant manager in a men's clothing store. He hopes to enter community college on a part time basis so that he can increase his knowledge of business and management.

SAMUEL

Samuel is in his thirties and was diagnosed several years ago as having learning disabilities and attention deficit disorder.

Samuel played sports in high school and won a scholarship to college. He did well but had to put in a great deal of effort. He served as an air force officer for over seven years and achieved the rank of Captain. He found the military to be a comfortable place and was proud of his accomplishments.

Still, he had always wanted to be a lawyer. He decided to take the Law School Admission Test. He did poorly. With tutoring, he was finally able to score well enough to gain admission to law school. After initially struggling in law school, he went for psychoeducational testing and was diagnosed as having auditory processing difficulties and ADD. This was a painful revelation. He did not like having a disability. At first, he resisted learning about it and sought to go forward as he always had in the past - without special help. Slowly, he became comfortable with a new view of himself. He sought advice as to helpful strategies and accommodations and began taking stimulant medication. He found that he was able to focus better, and his performance improved considerably. He is looking forward to practicing law. He feels that writing is a strong point for him, that he works well under pressure and that law practice will be stimulating and enjoyable for him.

CARLOS

Carlos is in his forties and has known since his early years in school that he has great difficulty in math (discalcula). Several years ago he learned that he also has attention deficit disorder.

Carlos is quick to point out that he "loved learning but hated school." It was miserable, but he struggled through, taking Algebra I twice but still never grasping it. He completed high school and one year of community college, where he took technical courses. Then he was drafted into the military. He found that he was able to learn better in the military than he had in school and attributes this to the short term objectives in the military, which enabled him to "see where it was going."

Employment for others did not work well for Carlos. He had trouble with social aspects, felt that he needed flexibility and could not tolerate constant deadlines. He loved to be creative with physical objects and in writing. He wanted to set his own pace and have great variety. Also, he simply by nature was an entrepreneurial type.

Soon he founded a business that used his talents and involved a long time interest of his: customizing automobiles. It quickly evolved into several businesses: automobile customizing and restoration, auto parts and writing and publishing newsletters dealing with automobile topics. Financial areas remain weak for him. He has this handled by an accountant and bookkeeper so that he is free to spend his time on what he does best and enjoys. Long-term planning for the business is an area of difficulty for him. Since he recognizes this, Carlos has retained a consultant with this specialty to assist him. In this way, Carlos is able to keep focused and enjoy his flourishing business.

C. SUMMARY

What do we learn from these experiences? The main point is that whatever one's disabilities may be, persistence is a key element of ultimate success. This does not always mean persistence in a particular job. It may mean leaving one job and moving on to one that is a better match. At times, there may be painful setbacks.To be able to persist to the maximum extent, an individual must know himself - the strengths and the deficits - and believe in himself.

8.

RELATED ISSUES

Patricia H. Latham, J.D.
Kathleen G. Nadeau, Ph.D.

A. INTRODUCTION

The individual with disabilities must also cope with many other issues in his life as he is seeking to succeed in the workplace. We will consider a few of those issues that relate to the workplace.

B. CAREER COUNSELING

The adult with ADD/LD may need career counseling prior to entering the workplace initially or at any point thereafter. The usual role of career counselor is to evaluate interests, abilities and personality type, guiding the individual toward broad clusters of careers for which he may be best suited. The career counselor specializing in ADD/LD should fulfill these traditional functions, however, the counselor also needs to consider the variety of ways that attention deficits and learning disabilities affect performance on the job. It is important that the career counselor appreciate the chronic emotional toll "invisible disabilities" may take on an individual. A good ADD/LD career counselor should not only provide information and guidance, but should also help with developing a more positive and adaptive attitude toward abilities in the workplace. The career counselor, in addition to suggesting career directions, should also provide a comprehensive list of specific, practical recommendations. These recommendations might include: particular types of testing, continuing education and training, strategies to be used in the workplace and accommodations that might be requested from employers.

Many possible strategies and accommodations are discussed in Chapter 3. Testing and continuing education and training are discussed below.

C. TESTING

The matter of testing may arise at several points throughout life in the workplace. The first may be upon making the transition from school to the workplace. There may be subsequent occasions, such as in connection with a job change or a contemplated career change.

Types of testing include ability, personality and interest.

Ability testing is of key importance. Most individuals have experienced this type of testing in moving through the educational system. Ability testing may be helpful in developing a realistic view of one's strengths and deficits in the workplace. Cognitive ability testing may range from an intelligence test such as the WAIS-R to a comprehensive psychoeducational test battery or neuropsychological test battery. They seek to measure specific cognitive abilities that impact upon our functioning in educational and work environments. Cognitive ability testing is especially important for individuals considering continuing education.

There are also batteries of ability tests which involve a much broader range of tasks than those related to intelligence or academically related skills. Much research exists on ability clusters measured by these test batteries as they relate to job match. Taking one of these ability tests can be very useful in charting a career direction.

A second type of testing is **personality testing**. Personality factors play a role in determining whether or not an individual is suited to a particular type of work. A personality test which may be helpful in career evaluation is the Meyers-Briggs Type Indicator (MBTI). Others include: California Psychological Inventory (CPI), Sixteen Personality Factor Questionnaire (16PF) and Gilford-Zimmerman Temperament Survey (GZTS). Other personality tests may be used to screen for psychiatric conditions that may on occasion accompany a learning disability or attention deficit disorder. Such accompanying conditions are often termed co-morbid conditions. They may include: depression, anxiety, bi-polar disorder and obsessive-compulsive disorder. One test often used to screen for these conditions is the Minnesota Multiphasic Personality Inventory-2 (MMPI-2).

The third type of testing is **interest testing**. An individual with a learning or attention disability is far more likely to develop and maintain the requisite motivation to succeed if he is truly interested in doing his work. For individuals with ADD who find work that is highly stimulating for them, it may be the first time that their attention is consistently drawn to what they are in fact supposed to be doing! Thus, interest testing may prove very helpful. Generally, interest tests indicate how interests which the individual reports match with particular fields. The following tests are often used: Self Directed Search (Holland, 1979), Vocational Preference Inventory (Holland, 1985) and the Strong Vocational Interest Blank (Campbell & Hansen, 1981).

Where can ADD and LD individuals go for testing?

If funds are available, testing may be arranged through various professionals specializing in these disabilities, including career counselors, neuropsychologists, psychologists and educational diagnostic specialists.

If funds are not available for testing, there are options. Some testing is available at no cost for those individuals who are still in the school system. For those who are beyond the school years, some may obtain helpful testing in connection with seeking entry into the armed forces, including reserve and national guard programs. Others may obtain testing and other assistance through their local rehabilitative services program, usually called the vocational rehabilitation office.

This is a state/federal program which assists individuals who have a physical or mental impairment that constitutes or results in a substantial impediment to employment. The evaluation phase of the program includes medical evaluation to determine the disability and vocational evaluation which may include testing.

D. CONTINUING EDUCATION AND TRAINING

Continuing education and training may facilitate success in the workplace, either prior to one's first job placement or at any time thereafter. The purpose may be remediation in a deficit area or career-related education/training.

Remediation is the process of improving skills in areas of deficit. This may include vision training, speech and language therapy or educational classes or tutoring in reading, writing, mathematics or memory.

Career related education/training may range from a minor commitment such as a computer course to provide the skills for an entry level computer job to a major commitment such as entering law school.

Remember that adults with attention deficit disorder and learning disabilities continue to mature and develop in their twenties and thirties. An educational pursuit that may have been overwhelming earlier may become manageable later.

Where are these educational and training opportunities? The answer is that they are widely available in many communities: colleges and universities, community colleges, technical schools, special adult remedial classes available through some learning disability schools and centers, and short term training courses leading to certification in specific areas (e.g. a television technician certificate through a community television training course and training leading to certification in security).

Training may be available through the local vocational rehabilitation office. Generally, an individual is eligible for services when (1) there is a documented physical, mental or emotional disability, (2) the disability limits ability to find, get or hold a job and (3) there is a good chance that vocational rehabilitation services can help with finding and keeping a job.

For eligible individuals, planning with a counselor will involve a review of test results to determine strengths and limitations. An Individualized Written Rehabilitation Program (IWRP) will be developed to help with finding and keeping a job. The IWRP may include: type of job, services needed to prepare, agreement on who will pay, date services will begin and ways to determine if services are helping with preparation for the job.

Vocational rehabilitation services may include: counseling and guidance, services and equipment for specific disabilities, vocational training to develop a skill, tools and equipment needed for the job, job placement services and follow up services.

There are additional community resources in many areas. Some corporations have programs to train and hire individuals with disabilities. There are organizations to assist with job placement and follow up, such as Electronic Industries Foundation.

E. PERSONAL FINANCIAL AND TAX PLANNING

The presence of a learning disability and attention deficit disorder may be a factor in personal, financial and tax planning. In this Chapter, we seek to provide some helpful tips.

1. PERSONAL AND FINANCIAL PLANNING

In planning investments, it may be advisable to tailor the investment recommendations to the particular abilities and disabilities of the individual. It is advisable to seek the advice of a financial planner with knowledge of disability issues. We will make a few suggestions for consideration.

For example, in the case of an adult individual with learning disabilities impacting upon his ability to organize and deal with calculations or lengthy written material, it may be wise to consider investments that are easy to manage.

One example would be a treasury direct account. This is an account with the U.S. Treasury in which one may directly purchase from the treasury, bonds or notes. There is no fee. There is no certificate. The interest is automatically electronically transferred to the holder's bank account, which is designated on the form submitted to the Bureau of the Public Debt of the U. S. Treasury. There are periodic statements which show the holdings. As bonds or notes become due, a form is sent to the holder. If no action is taken the principal is transferred to the holder's bank account. If a reinvestment box is checked and the form returned to the Treasury, then the principal is rolled over into the designated bond or note. It should also be noted that interest on Treasury obligations is not taxable by the states.

If there is a desire to consider stocks, corporate bonds and municipal bonds, again it would seem advisable to select high quality securities with a good return. Speculative securities would involve risk and require more attention to management.

Securities may be purchased through mutual funds. This permits diversification and professional management. Once the investment is made, there are periodic statements. There are load funds and no load funds, The load is essentially a marketing commission. The load is often a front end load or up front percentage (usually between 4% and 8.5%) of the total amount invested. Load funds are usually purchased through brokers.

A convenient vehicle for maintaining investments which one wishes directly to hold, such as stocks, corporate bonds and municipal bonds, is a comprehensive account with a brokerage house. The account may be called an asset account or a cash management account. There may be an annual fee for the account. The account may hold various securities and cash and offer a credit card and checking account. The advantage is simplicity. All organizing and calculating is done by the brokerage house. Each month the investor receives a statement showing the holdings, their values, the income generated, the cash balance, the checks written and the credit card transactions. It is not necessary to send a check to pay the credit card bill, as the amount is automatically debited against the account.

Another means of simplifying finances is to have automatic drafting of the checking account for mortgage, medical insurance and other payments and automatic deposit to the checking account of pay checks and Treasury interest.

For long term purposes, it may be advisable to establish an Individual Retirement Account, and place in it annually the allowed amount, thus building assets for retirement and creating a tax deduction.

As is generally advisable for most people, consideration should be given to executing a will, a durable power of attorney, a living will and a designation of health care surrogate. The person named in the durable power of attorney may assist in handling the affairs of the individual with the disability. The power of attorney may be immediately in effect or may be "stand by" to come into effect in the event that the individual is no longer able to act.

Insurance is an important issue. Generally, it is advisable for individuals with learning disabilities and attention deficit disorder to have insurance, including life, disability and medical insurance. Even if the individual is working and has medical insurance through his employer, it may be advisable to carry back-up medical insurance, perhaps with a very high deductible to keep the premium to a minimum.

2. TAX PLANNING

The individual with a disability may receive income but have reduced income or periods of unemployment because of his disability. If so, the tax laws apply to him as they would to anyone receiving income.

Certain expenses in connection with treating or alleviating a mental or physical disability may be deductible as medical expenses. Handicaps for purposes of the medical expense deduction include: neurological disorders, emotional and psychological disorders and sometimes learning disabilities. It is important to keep in mind that one can't cure a learning disability or attention deficit disorder as one might cure an infection. Still, there are approaches that alleviate these disabilities and treat related conditions.

Expenses for individuals with these disabilities which have been held deductible under certain circumstances include: tuition for a school specializing in learning disabilities, the cost of tutoring, fees for psychological counseling, fees for special diagnostic testing and necessary special equipment, such as a tape recorder.

Remember that each individual with a disability is unique, and the validity of the deduction depends upon the particular facts. To support the deduction, it is advisable to take several steps: have recent testing documenting the disabilities, have a recent professional opinion recommending the course of action leading to the medical expense and have clear and detailed documentation of the expense.

We have sought to provide a starting point in planning. This is not comprehensive or applicable to a particular set of circumstances. We recommend professional advice for each particular case.

F. SUMMARY

The adult with ADD/LD may consider career counseling, various types of testing and continuing education to help with progressing in the workplace. Personal financial and tax planning are also influenced by the presence of a disability. Proper planning may free up time and energy needed in the workplace and make maximum use of income earned in the workplace.

9.

LEGAL RIGHTS

Peter S. Latham, J.D.
Patricia H. Latham, J.D.

A. INTRODUCTION

No book about the workplace is complete without a discussion of legal rights. In the text that follows, we have attempted to simplify the discussion of the legal principles, constitutional requirements, statutes, regulations and interpretive rulings of federal agencies. The result is a text which is more readable but more general than most legal texts. The following discussion should not be considered legal advice which is applicable to particular cases. For that, you should obtain the services of counsel. This Chapter provides a starting point and basic language to assist you.

B. BASIC PRINCIPLES, THE CONSTITUTION AND STATUTES

1. THE CONSTITUTION

The 5th and 14th amendments to the Constitution are the most important source of the rights of individuals with disabilities. The 14th Amendment provides in pertinent part that "No State shall ... deny to any person within its jurisdiction the equal protection of the laws" or "deprive any person of life, liberty, or property, without due process of law." Section 5 of the 14th Amendment provides that the

"Congress shall have the power to enforce, by appropriate legislation, the provisions of this article." The 5th Amendment contains the identical due process language and has incorporated the "equal protection" concept.

Modern concepts of due process and equal protection for individuals with disabilities evolved directly from the requirement of equal access to education. While the states have no constitutional obligation to provide free public education, all states do, and when they do, that education must be available to all. *Brown v. Board of Education,* 347 U.S. 483 (1954) While *Brown* is cited primarily for its racial classification holding, it also stands for the proposition that the equal right to an education is a fundamental human right. The Court said:

> In these days, it is doubtful that any child may reasonably be expected to succeed in life if he is denied the opportunity of an education. Such an opportunity, where the state has undertaken to provide it, is a right which must be made available to all on equal terms. 347 U.S. 483, at 493

The equal "fundamental rights" analysis of *Brown* has been followed in landmark constitutional cases involving individuals with disabilities.

Equal protection of the law for persons with disabilities means an equal opportunity to obtain the same result, to gain the same benefit, or to reach the same level of achievement, as non-disabled persons in the most integrated setting appropriate to the person's needs. However, employment, education, housing, aids, benefits, and services, to be equally accessible, need not necessarily produce the identical result or level of achievement for handicapped and non-handicapped persons.

The Constitutional requirements of due process and equal protection are made specific and uniform by statutes which are authorized by, and implement these Constitutional provisions. In general, statutes do one of three things, they 1] prohibit discrimination 2] require affirmative action or 3] provide funds for specific activities and programs. In the latter case, the recipient is required to agree that it will conduct its programs without discrimination.

2. FEDERAL STATUTORY LAW

a. The IDEA

The Individuals With Disabilities Education Act (20 U.S.C. §1400 *et seq.*) (IDEA), in general, mandates that public schools districts receiving federal funds, must provide a "free appropriate public education" (FAPE) to children with disabilities. Many of the readers of this book have either themselves benefitted from this statute or know someone who did. But, while the IDEA is best known for its educational requirements, it also contains provisions mandating that school district recipients employ affirmative action methods in employment as well. *Fitzgerald v. Green Valley Area Education Agency*, 589 F. Supp. 1130 (S.D. Iowa 1984) Moreover, the IDEA [(20 U.S.C. §1401 (a) (15)] contains a definition of "children with specific learning disabilities" which is helpful and influential in interpreting the Rehabilitation Act of 1973 and the Americans with Disabilities Act.

b. The Rehabilitation Act of 1973

The Rehabilitation Act of 1973 (29 U.S.C. § 701 *et seq.*) (RA) essentially outlaws discrimination against individuals with disabilities in education, employment (including federal government employment), and access to the benefits of federal programs by federal agencies and federal grant and contract recipients. In general, the statute applies only to: a] the federal government b] federal government contractors and c] federal grant recipients. In the first two cases, the RA requires affirmative action. In the third it does not.

c. The Americans with Disabilities Act

The Americans with Disabilities Act (42 U.S.C. § 12101 *et seq.*) (ADA) outlaws discrimination against individuals with disabilities in private sector employment, state and local government employment, state and local government activities and programs, and public accommodations. Additionally, it extends the protections of the RA to individuals with disabilities who are employed by the Congress. Unlike the RA, the ADA's protections do not depend on the receipt of federal funds. Affirmative action is not required of any activities subject to the ADA.

3. THE RIGHT TO BE FREE FROM DISCRIMINATION

a. Overview

In order to obtain the protections of the RA or ADA, it is necessary to establish that: 1] you are an "individual with a disability," **and** 2] you are "otherwise qualified," **and** 3] you were denied a job, education, or other benefit "solely by reason" of the disability; **and** 4] the individual, firm, or governmental agency which refused you is covered by the RA or ADA. *Fitzgerald v. Green Valley Area Education Agency,* 589 F. Supp. 1130 (S.D. Iowa 1984) We will consider each of these in turn.

The bar against employment discrimination covers all employment activities of the firms to which it applies. The Code of Federal Regulations contains a comprehensive list of activities which may not be undertaken in a discriminatory manner. The bar against discrimination applies to recruitment, advertising and job application procedures, hiring, upgrading, promotion, award of tenure, demotion, transfer, layoff, termination, right of return from layoff, rehiring, rates of pay, compensation, changes in compensation, job assignments, job classifications, organizational structures, position descriptions, lines of progression, seniority lists, leaves of absence, sick leave, other leaves, fringe benefits, selection and financial support for training, including apprenticeships, professional meetings, conferences, and other related activities, selection for leaves of absence to pursue training, activities sponsored by a covered entity including social and recreational programs and any other term, condition, or privilege of employment. [29 CFR ¶¶1630.4 (a)-(i)].

The prohibitions against discrimination are intended to be administered on a case by case basis. This means that each of the elements discussed below must be considered as they apply to the facts of an individual case. Consequently, the process of invoking the right to be free from discrimination by reason of a disability can be an extensive one.

b. Individual with a Disability

Under both the RA and ADA, an "individual with a disability" is "any individual who:

> (i) has a physical or mental impairment which substantially limits one or more of such person's major life activities,
> (ii) has a record of such an impairment, or
> (iii) is regarded as having such an impairment.
> 29 U.S.C. § 706(8)(B).

The second and third definitions are intended to protect individuals who 1] previously had a disability but do not now and 2] are treated as though they had a disability but do not. The most important category for our purposes is the first, and it is discussed below. The ADA contains definitions which are "equivalent" to those contained in the RA. The discussion which follows applies to both statutes unless otherwise specified.

1. Impairments Covered

The definition of a "physical or mental impairment" includes: "any mental or psychological disorder, such as mental retardation, organic brain syndrome, emotional or mental illness, and specific learning disabilities." 29 CFR § 1613.702(b)(2). This formulation appears in a great many regulations. Note that "specific learning disabilities" are expressly covered by the regulations. The Appendix to Part 1630 of Title 29 of the Code of Federal Regulations (which is entitled INTERPRETIVE GUIDANCE ON TITLE I OF THE AMERICANS WITH DISABILITIES ACT) provides, for example, that a lack of education is not considered a disability. It then states:

> However, an individual who is unable to read because of dyslexia would be an individual with a disability because dyslexia, a learning disability, is an impairment.
> (INTERPRETIVE GUIDANCE at 404)

ADD is not specifically mentioned in the regulations. ADD, however, has been recognized as a "mental or psychological disorder." In *Letter of Findings (LOF) OCR Docket No. 04-90-1617; 17 Sep 90; Gaston County School District* the Department of Education's Office of Civil Rights ruled that the Gaston County School District of North Carolina (which received federal funding) failed to identify, evaluate, and provide the complainant's ADD child with a free public education appropriate to his disorder and thereby violated the RA. (29 U.S.C. § 794). There are similar holdings under the ADA.

Of special importance to individuals with ADD is the requirement that the effects of medication are not to be considered in assessing whether an individual has an "impairment." The INTERPRETIVE GUIDANCE provides:

> The existence of an impairment is to be determined without regard to mitigating measures such as medicines.... For example, an individual with epilepsy would be considered to have an impairment even if the symptoms of the disorder were completely controlled by medicine .... (INTERPRETIVE GUIDANCE at 402)

The severity of one's ADD must therefore be evaluated without considering the beneficial effects of medications such as those discussed by Dr. Quinn in Chapter 1 above.

Thus, the RA and ADA potentially apply to individuals with learning disabilities and attention deficit disorder. However, the LD or ADD in question must also substantially limit a major life activity.

2. Substantially Limits

The impact of the disability must be severe enough to result in actual substandard performance. The regulations provide that the term "substantially limits" means **either** that an individual is 1] "[u]nable to perform a major life activity that the average person in the general population can perform" or 2] is "[s]ignificantly restricted as to the condition, manner or duration" of the major life activity in question, when measured against the abilities of the "average person in the general population." [29 CFR ¶¶ 1630.2(j)(1)(i)-(ii)] In assessing the impact of limitations, the following factors must also be considered: 1] the nature and severity of the impairment 2] the actual or expected duration of the impairment and the permanent or long term impact of the impairment. [29 CFR ¶¶ 1630.2(j)(2)(i)-(iii)]

Proof of adverse impact is required even where learning is involved. For example, in one case, an ADD child who struggled with his work but whose classroom performance was adequate, and who exhibited no disruptive behavior was found not to have a disability which interfered with learning! *(See Letter of Findings (LOF) Docket No. 15-93-1016; 23 Mar 1993; Forest Hills Local School District)*

Therefore, any presentation to an employer should address in detail the nature and severity of the LD or ADD and its specific impact on the individual's ability to perform the essential features of a particular job. Chapters 1 and 2 provide comprehensive descriptions of the specific ways in which ADD and LD can present.

3. Major Life Activities

There are specific guidelines which address whether an impairment substantially limits a major life activity and how that limitation is measured. The EEOC has issued regulations which require a two step test in determining whether a major life activity has been substantially limited.

The major life tasks are considered to be caring for oneself, performing manual tasks, walking, seeing, hearing, speaking, breathing, learning, and working. [29 CFR ¶ 1630.2(i)] **Note** that the regulations provide that learning and working are major life activities, and these are the ones that most concern us. However, working is treated differently from all other major life activities for purposes of considering whether an individual with an impairment is substantially limited. In order to determine whether a substantial limitation on **working** exists, the INTERPRETIVE GUIDANCE requires that the following additional factors be considered: 1] the geographical area to which the individual has reasonable access 2] the number and types of jobs utilizing similar training, knowledge, skills or abilities within the geographical area from which the individual is disqualified and 3] the number and types of jobs **not** utilizing similar training, knowledge, skills or abilities within the geographical area from which the individual is also disqualified. [29 CFR ¶¶ 1630.2(j)(3)(ii)] These tests are required to ensure that the individual with a disability is barred from significant **classes** of jobs, and not just **a particular** job. Only disabilities with the former (and broader) impact are considered substantially to limit working. The decided cases have reached similar results. In *Macaranas v. United States Postal Service, 48 MSPR 323 (1991)* the Merit Systems Protection Board held that, in assessing whether there is a substantial limitation on working, one should consider 1] the type of work involved 2] the number of jobs barred and 3] number of jobs barred in the geographical area to which there is reasonable access.

In *Daley v. Koch, et al.*, 892 F.2d 212 (2nd Cir. 1989), the court held that an applicant for a police officer's job who passed the New York Civil Service examination could be rejected where psychological testing and interviews showed him to have poor judgement, irresponsible behavior and poor impulse control but no "psychological disease or disorder." In so ruling, the court held that, while working is a major life activity, police work, or any specific job was not. Therefore, reasoned the court, there was no impairment of a major life activity.

In *Joyner v. Department of the Navy*, 47 MSPR 596 (1991), a machinist whose back injury prevented him from performing normal physical movements, but not clerical work, was substantially limited in his occupation as a laborer. However, a stock clerk whose job is to manage an inventory of toxic chemicals is not substantially limited in his occupation if he is allergic to and unable to work with particular chemicals. *Vernon v. Veteran's Administration,* 54 MSPR 486 (1992)

Consideration of the impact on working need not be undertaken where a substantial impact on another major life activity can be shown.

> If an individual is not substantially limited with respect to any other major life activity, the individual's ability to perform the major life activity of working should be considered. If an individual is substantially limited in any other major life activity, no determination should be made as to whether the individual is substantially limited in working. For example, if an individual is blind, *i.e.*, substantially limited in the major life activity of seeing, there is no need to determine whether the individual is also substantially limited in the major life activity of working. The determination of whether an individual is substantially limited in working must also be

made on a case by case basis. (INTERPRETIVE GUIDANCE at 404)

Therefore, it is important to analyze the impact of a disability on each of the major life activities in addition to working when assessing the impact of the RA and ADA. In the cases of ADD and LD, the disabilities are ordinarily present from birth and, in most cases, have had a severe impact on learning and socialization (arguably an element of caring for oneself) long before adulthood. Because this is so, there is frequently a substantial record from which impact can be demonstrated. Where a diagnosis is made later in life, substantial impact can be shown by educational and psychological testing.

c. Otherwise Qualified

Under both the RA and ADA, an "individual with a disability" must be one who is "otherwise qualified." An "otherwise qualified" individual is one who, though possessed of a disability, would be eligible for the job, education, or program benefit, with or without a reasonable accommodation. The institution or employer must either provide the accommodation or justify in detail the refusal to provide it. *Fitzgerald v. Green Valley Area Education Agency,* 589 F. Supp. 1130 (S.D. Iowa 1984)

1. Reasonable Accommodations

Reasonable accommodations are of three general types: 1] those required to ensure equal opportunity in the job application process 2] those which enable the individual with a disability to perform the essential features of a job and 3] those which enable individuals with disabilities to enjoy the same benefits and privileges as those available to individuals without disabilities. (INTERPRETIVE GUIDANCE at 408) Reasonable accommodations for ADD and LD can include any of the following:

- providing or modifying equipment or devices,
- job restructuring,
- part-time or modified work schedules,
- reassignment to a vacant position,

- adjusting or modifying examinations, training materials, or policies,
- providing readers or interpreters, and
- making the workplace readily accessible to and usable by people with disabilities.

U.S. Equal Employment Opportunity Commission, THE AMERICANS WITH DISABILITIES ACT; YOUR RIGHTS AS AN INDIVIDUAL WITH A DISABILITY; EEOC-BK-18 (1991)

Note: Job reassignment may be required generally only under the ADA. It is not required by "Section 504" of the RA.

Despite this sweeping description, the accommodations actually required for individuals with ADD and LD are generally not extensive or expensive. The President's Committee on Employment of People with Disabilities has pointed out:

- Thirty-one percent of accommodations cost nothing.
- Fifty percent cost less than $50.00.
- Sixty-nine percent cost less than $500.00
- Eighty-eight percent cost less than $1,000.00.

JOB ACCOMMODATION IDEAS, President's Committee on Employment of People with Disabilities; October 1993

The President's Commission gave these examples which may be helpful.

Problem: A person with a learning disability worked in the mail room and had difficulty remembering which streets belonged to which zip codes.

Solution: A rolodex card system was filed by street name alphabetically with the zip code. This helped him to increase his output. ($150.00)

***

Problem: An individual with dyslexia who worked as a police officer spent hours filling out forms at the end of each day.

Solution: He was provided with a tape recorder. A secretary typed out his reports from dictation, while she typed others from handwritten copy. This accommodation allowed him to keep his job. ($69.00)

JOB ACCOMMODATION IDEAS; President's Committee on Employment of People with

The EEOC recommends a four step process in determining whether a reasonable accommodation is required.

1] Analyze the particular job involved and determine its purpose and essential functions.

2] Consult with the individual with a disability to ascertain the precise job-related limitations imposed by the individual's disability and how those limitations could be overcome with a reasonable accommodation;

3] In consultation with the individual to be accommodated, identify potential accommodations and assess the effectiveness each would have in enabling the individual to perform the essential functions of the position; and

4] Consider the preference of the individual to be accommodated and select and implement the accommodation that is most appropriate for both the employee and employer. (INTERPRETIVE GUIDANCE at 415)

Note the central role played by the definition of the essential features of the job. Essential features are discussed below.

While federal law contains little guidance concerning the specific reasonable accommodations for LD/ADD individuals, it appears probable that the following would be required in appropriate cases: 1] providing a structured learning/working environment 2] repeating and simplifying instructions about work assignments 3] supplementing verbal instructions with visual instructions 4] adjusting class or work schedules 5] modifying test delivery 6] using tape recorders and computer - aided instruction or work methods and 7] other audio-visual equipment. These accommodations track closely those outlined in the Memorandum, Office of Special Education and Rehabilitative Services, issued by the Department of Education on 16 September 1991 as guidance to school districts in educating children with ADD under the IDEA. Many specific accommodations are described in Chapter 3.

2. Undue Hardship

A "reasonable accommodation" is one which does not either 1] alter the essential nature of a job or 2] result in "significant difficulty or expense" to the employer. A proposed accommodation which does either of these things creates an "undue hardship" and need not be made. (INTERPRETIVE GUIDANCE at 409)

In judging whether a proposed accommodation creates an "undue hardship," the particular circumstances of the employer's situation must be considered. What is an undue hardship for one employer may not be an undue hardship for another. The EEOC gives as an example, the case of an individual with a disabling visual impairment that makes it extremely difficult to see in dim lighting. If such an individual were to seek employment as a waiter in a nightclub, the club would not be required to provide bright lighting for the dining and lounge areas even though it would involve nothing more than turning up the lights. The nightclub relies on dim lighting to create an "ambiance" which attracts customers, and bright lighting would destroy the nightclub's trade. Providing it would be an undue hardship. (INTERPRETIVE GUIDANCE at 409)

The courts have performed similar analyses. In *Fitzgerald v. Green Valley Area Education Agency*, 589 F. Supp. 1130 (S.D. Iowa 1984), the Court held that a school district's requirement that all teachers take turns driving school busses was not an essential part of the teaching function. Accordingly, the school district was required to restructure its job requirements to permit the hiring of a qualified teacher whose dyslexia and other impairments prevented him from driving a school bus.

However, in another case, the Court held that dispatcher duties which were required of all firemen on a rotational basis and involved the use of computers were an essential part of the work of a fireman and refused to order job restructuring. The United States Court of Appeals for the Second Circuit affirmed the trial court. *DiPompo v. West Point Military Academy, et al.*, 960 F.2d 326 (2nd Cir. 1992)

A major factor in deciding whether a particular proposed accommodation is reasonable, is the potential burden on the employer. In *Lynch v. Department of Education* 52 MSPR 541 (1992), a GS-13 Trial Attorney was dismissed for unsatisfactory work and excessive absences due to an epileptic condition which was treatable with medication. The medication, however, affected her memory and ability to concentrate. As a reasonable accommodation she requested 1] training in legal drafting 2] specific structured assignments including clear written assignment instructions and increased supervisory assistance and 3] the opportunity to make up hours missed by late arrivals. These accommodations were found to be reasonable, in our view because they increased only marginally, if at all, the burden on the employer. Specifically, the agency needed legal drafting done. Further, it already had in place supervisors whose very purpose was to make sure that work flowed smoothly. Finally, the opportunity to make up missed work functioned very much like the flex-time program many employers (including the agency) already had in place. As a result, the individual was found to be a "qualified handicapped person" under the RA whose proposed accommodation was reasonable and was ordered reinstated.

d. Solely By Reason Of

An individual with a disability must also show that he or she has been denied employment, education or access to a public accommodation solely by reason of the disability. In *Ross v. Beaumont Hospital et al.* 687 F. Supp. 1115 (E.D. Mich.1988) a hospital terminated the privileges of a surgeon who suffered from narcolepsy despite the fact that her narcolepsy was largely controlled through medication. However, the surgeon also engaged in verbal abuse of nurses over a seven year period. There was no evidence that the abuse was related to the narcolepsy. Accordingly, the termination was held to be lawful under the RA because it was based in major part on her unacceptable conduct.

e. The RA or the ADA Applies

Finally, an individual with a disability must show that the RA or ADA is applicable to his or her case. The RA is closely similar to the ADA in that both outlaw discrimination against persons with disabilities in employment, education and access to publicly available programs. The RA differs from the ADA in three principal respects, however. First, the RA follows federal dollars. It applies to the federal government, federal government contractors, and federal grant recipients. In the case of contractors and grant recipients, compliance with the RA is a condition of receiving federal contracts and grants. The ADA applies directly and its application does not depend on the agreement of the recipient. Second, the RA requires affirmative action in federal government and government contractor employment, while the ADA does not. Third, the ADA applies to virtually all public accommodations while the RA does not.

f. Individualized Inquiry

The "bottom line" of all these requirements is simply this: is the individual whose disability substantially limits a major life activity qualified for the education or job he or she seeks with or without a reasonable accommodation? In order to answer this question, businesses, educational institutions, licensing authorities, and firms offering public accommodations must undertake an "individualized inquiry" whose purpose is to consider whether this individual's impairment can be accommodated without undue hardship, or the elimination of essential job requirements. The process is intended to ensure that (in our context) employment decisions are made for sound reasons and not on the basis of hatred, fears, or the application of stereotypes. *Ward v. Skinner,* 943 F.2d 157 (1st Cir. 1991), *cert. denied*, 188 L.E.2d 207 (1992) In making these judgements, the courts will give great weight to 1] the nature of the job 2] the level of the job 3] whether the public safety is directly or indirectly involved and 4] whether the proposed accommodation is substantially similar to activities already required of or undertaken by the employer.

4. AFFIRMATIVE ACTION

The duty to undertake affirmative action differs from the duty to avoid discrimination. Affirmative action is the positive obligation to adopt and implement a plan (acceptable to the government) for the employment of individuals with disabilities. It is required of 1] the federal government 2] federal government contractors and 3] some recipients of federal funding under the IDEA. In contrast, the duty to avoid discrimination is the obligation to refrain from discriminatory conduct.

C. SPECIFIC PROBLEMS

1. WHAT IS A JOB?

To begin with, it is important to consider just what we mean by job requirements. Most job "requirements" fall into at least 6 separate categories. These are 1] academic qualifications 2] required on-the-job experience 3] competence in the work itself 4] general standards of cooperativeness in the work situation 5] compliance with "good citizenship" rules - e.g. being on time; no unauthorized absences, etc. and 6] a record which is free from convictions for offenses whose commission suggests dishonesty, or unreliability. Moreover, requirements 3-5 become increasingly subjective as the seniority and pay of the positions increase. All of these factors must be considered in selecting a job and deciding whether and how to deal with a disability.

In *Dazey v. Department of the Air Force,* 54 MSPR 658 (1992), a GS-12 auditor was removed in major part for using abusive language in the office. She suffered from mood changes caused by manic depression and an "apparently irrational dislike for her supervisor." Her psychiatrist prescribed lithium and prozac and testified that the treatment would prevent bizarre disruptive behavior if the auditor returned to the workplace even without accommodations. However, the auditor displayed some of these symptoms at the trial notwithstanding medication. The Administrative Judge found that she had not shown that medication was a sufficient answer. Accordingly, the Judge found that she "could not perform the essential functions of her position because such essential functions included not engaging in the bizarre behavior previously engaged in, and getting along with her supervisor." Clearly, having the 1] academic qualifications 2] required on-the-job experience and 3] competence in the work itself, while failing to meet general standards of cooperativeness in the work situation and comply with "good citizenship" rules, was not sufficient.

2. ESSENTIAL FEATURES

All of these six elements may be considered essential features of jobs. As noted above, meeting general standards and rules becomes increasingly important as the seniority of the position increases. However, these elements can be highly subjective, and in some cases, can serve as a pretext for discrimination. The regulations and EEOC INTERPRETIVE GUIDANCE analyze the essential features of a job by considering three factors:

> The first factor is whether the position exists to perform a particular function....
>
> The second factor in determining whether a function is essential is the number of other employees available to perform that job function or among whom the performance of that job function can be distributed....
>
> The third factor is the degree of expertise or skill required to perform the function. (INTERPRETIVE GUID-

Note that the EEOC approach is to consider primarily the role the job plays in the employer's operations rather than the individual attributes necessary to perform the job. However, the case law suggests that the broader factors considered in this section also apply.

An individual with a disability is required to perform the essential features of a job with or without a reasonable accommodation. All job features which are not essential are considered marginal, and therefore capable of being restructured as a reasonable accommodation.

3. JOB ADVERTISING

The employment process usually begins with an advertisement. While the ADA does not require that job descriptions be written, a well established job description, whose terms are reflected in the advertising, can be important evidence in deciding whether a particular feature of the job is essential. Therefore, as a practical matter, the job advertisement should list only those job features which are essential. Moreover, reasonable accommodation in the job application process may be required.

4. HIRING AND TESTING

Testing is used for education, as well as job placement, retention, and advancement. Testing which relies on a single criterion is unlawful where that criterion can be shown to be an inaccurate predictor of performance. In *Stutts v. Freeman, et al,* 694 F.2d 666 (11th Cir. 1983), a dyslexic laborer applied for a job as a heavy equipment operator and was rejected solely on the basis of a low score on written tests, when independent tests showed he possessed an above average intelligence, coordination and aptitude for the apprenticeship training program. The 11th Circuit held that the Rehabilitation Act of 1973 had been violated, stating:

> When an employer like TVA chooses a test that discriminates against handicapped persons as its sole hiring criterion, and makes no meaningful accommodation for a handicapped applicant, it violates the Rehabilitation Act of 1973. 694 F.2d 666 at 669

The Law School Aptitude Tests (LSAT's) are potentially such a test for one with attentional and organizational problems. Accordingly, law schools, while they may require one to take the test (under modified conditions), are precluded from basing their acceptance decisions with respect to applicants with disabilities on those tests. Indeed, some law schools disregard the LSAT results entirely and base their acceptance decisions on 1] grade point averages 2] undergraduate transcripts and curricula 3] letters of recommendation and 4] LSAT writing samples. See *Letter of Findings (LOF) OCR Docket No. 02-91-2074; 5 Mar 1992; Cornell University Law School.*

The Regulations provide:

> It is unlawful for a covered entity to use qualification standards, employment tests or other selection criteria that screen out or tend to screen out an individual with a disability or a class of individuals with disabilities, on the basis of disability, unless the standard, test or other selection criteria, as used by the covered entity, is shown to be job-related for the position in question and is consistent with business necessity. [29 CFR § 1630.10]

In addition, an employer must:

> select and administer tests concerning employment in the most effective manner to ensure that, when a test is administered to a job applicant or employee who has a disability that impairs sensory, manual or speaking skills, the test results accurately reflect the skills, aptitude, or whatever other factor ... that the test purports to measure, rather than reflecting the impaired sensory, manual, or speaking skills of such employee or applicant (except where such skills are the factors that the test purports to measure.) [29 CFR § 1630.11]

These regulations are closely patterned on Department of Education guidelines [34 CFR §104.35] for testing in the context of the IDEA which are generally helpful in interpreting them. DOE requires that tests and other evaluation materials 1] must be "validated for the specific purpose for which they are used" 2] must be "administered by trained personnel" 3] must "include those tailored to assess specific areas of educational need" and 4] must produce "results" which "accurately reflect the student's aptitude or achievement level" rather than his or her "impaired sensory, manual, or speaking skills" unless specific justification is provided.

While use of a single testing criterion or method is suspect, it may be defensible where the aptitude measured is important to the educational institution or job requirements.

In *Wynne v. Tufts University School of Medicine,* 932 F.2d 19 (1st Cir. 1991) Wynne, a dyslexic student, was held to have been properly dismissed from medical school after failing numerous courses (including biochemistry - three times) during successive attempts to complete the first-year program. Tufts had refused him permission to take multiple choice examinations orally. On appeal from the District Court's rejection of Wynne's claim, the 1st Circuit reversed the District Court's determination, finding that the record did not show that alternative testing methods had been explored and found unsuitable (there was evidence that Brown University permitted oral testing in place of written multiple choice testing), or that Wynne's academic problems resulted from causes other than dyslexia. On remand, Tufts supplemented the record and showed that it "clearly evaluated alternatives to its current testing format and concluded change was not practicable." The District Court found in Tufts' favor, holding that Tufts' decision was rationally justified, and that the accommodations actually provided were reasonable, and the First Circuit affirmed that decision in *Wynne v. Tufts University School of Medicine,* 976 F.2d 791 (1st Cir. 1992). The United States Supreme Court refused to review this case when asked to do so, and consequently the lower court's ruling stands.

In *Pandazides v. Virginia Board of Education et al.,* 946 F.2d 345 (4th Cir. 1991), the courts considered the extent and nature of accommodations which could be extended to a learning disabled applicant for a teacher's certification. Pandazides was given a probationary certification which required that she pass the NTE. Pandazides was given accommodations by the NTE, none of which enabled her to pass the test. She then proposed that she be given as accommodations: 1] an untimed test and 2] the right to engage in discussions with the testing examiner about the test while taking it. Alternatively, she requested that the NTE be waived. No limit was place on the number of times she could take the test. She was denied all of these proposed modifications, brought suit under the RA and lost in the District Court. On appeal, the 4th Circuit reversed the trial court and remanded the case with instructions for the trial court to conduct an individualized inquiry as to 1] whether the NTE requirements were essential to the job 2] whether she could perform the essential functions of the position, and whether a 3] test waiver was a reasonable accommodation.

The District Court considered the case on remand in *Pandazides v. Virginia Board of Education,* 804 F. Supp. 794 (E.D. Va. 1992), and held that Pandazides was not an "otherwise qualified" individual with a disability because (among other things) her learning disabilities prevented her from meeting the essential requirements for a teaching position:

> Plaintiff is not 'otherwise qualified' under § 504 because she cannot perform 'essential functions' of public school teacher in Virginia. (sic) The ability to read intelligently, to comprehend written and spoken communication accurately, effectively and quickly, and to respond to written and spoken communication professionally, effectively and quickly, are 'essential functions' of a special education, public school teacher in Virginia. Moreover, the ability to manage a classroom is an 'essential function' for a public school teacher in grades 1 through 12 in Virginia. Plaintiff has failed to prove competence in this essential function." (804 F. Supp. 794 at 803)

Pandazides and *Wynne* show that the courts will give great deference to the judgement of those charged with testing and educating professionals, even when the academic requirements generated by that judgement are debatable.

5. PRE-EMPLOYMENT INQUIRIES

ADD and LD are disabilities different from many others. Unlike mobility, hearing, or speech impairment, they are not obvious on first meeting. Therefore an individual with ADD/LD is faced with the decision whether to declare his disability.

The EEOC advises as follows:

Q. Should I tell my employer that I have a disability?

A. If you think you will need a reasonable accommodation in order to participate in the application process or to perform essential job functions, you should inform the employer that an accommodation will be needed. Employers are required to provide reasonable accommodation only for the physical or mental limitations of a qualified individual with a disability of which they are aware. Generally, it is the responsibility of the employee to inform the employer that an accommodation is needed.

U.S. Equal Employment Opportunity Commission, THE AMERICANS WITH DISABILITIES ACT; YOUR RIGHTS AS AN INDIVIDUAL WITH A DISABILITY; EEOC-BK-18 (1991) at page 7

An employer may not require that an applicant for employment disclose the existence of a disability but may request information concerning an applicant's ability to perform the essential or marginal functions of the job under consideration prior to making an offer. [29 CFR § 1630.13] An employer may also provide that job offers be conditioned on post-offer medical examinations which will demonstrate the individual's suitability to perform the essential functions of a job. Finally, the employer may require a medical examination for the purpose of analyzing a request for reasonable accommodations if all entering employees in the same job category are required to answer the same questions and undergo the same examination. [29 CFR § 1630.14]

The consequences of **not** identifying an LD or ADD individual's disability may, in some cases, be severe, however. This is particularly true where diminished social skills form part of the disability. In *Mancini v. General Electric Co.*, 820 F. Supp. 141 (D. Vt. 1993), the court held that an employee with a disability who had developed a personality conflict with his supervisor resulting in a failure to comply with the supervisor's directions to work in particular places which made him uncomfortable, was properly discharged under the Vermont Fair Employment Practices Act (similar to the RA and ADA). The court held that the employer had no duty to transfer the employee in order to avoid a conflict with the supervisor. In so ruling, the court said that "[E]mployees must be present and willing to obey their supervisors to perform the essential functions of their job." [820 F. Supp. 141 at 147] Had the employee identified himself as an individual with a disability and employed the strategies discussed in Chapter 3, it is entirely possible that the work situation would not have deteriorated to the point of disobedience and firing.

6. DISPARATE TREATMENT AND IMPACT

An employer may not use selection procedures which 1] intentionally eliminate individuals with disabilities from the workforce, or which 2] while superficially neutral, have an adverse impact on an individual with a disability, or tend to screen out individuals with disabilities as a class unless (in the latter case) they are justified by business necessity. However, even in the latter case, business necessity cannot justify a restriction which can be overcome by a reasonable accommodation. In legal language, the first class of restrictions is termed intentional discrimination or "disparate treatment" while the second is called "disparate impact" discrimination. *McWright v. Alexander, et al.,* 982 F. 2d 222 (7th Cir. 1992)

D. ENFORCEMENT

1. REHABILITATION ACT OF 1973

The RA contains various enforcement mechanisms. Most importantly, (for our purposes) it may be enforced by civil suit, either by itself, or in appropriate cases, with civil rights statutes. Most private actions are for injunctive relief, whose purpose is to prevent discrimination or to correct its effects. Civil actions may also be brought by the United States for the same purpose. The Department of Justice can, in some cases, pursue fines and penalties. Individuals may recover attorneys' fees in appropriate cases.

2. AMERICANS WITH DISABILITIES ACT

The Act contains various enforcement mechanisms. These include actions by the EEOC, Justice Department as well as private actions.

The ADA enforcement provisions are borrowed from the Civil Rights Act of 1964. They permit civil suits by individuals for relief including: injunctive relief, back pay and sometimes, damages. However, the Department of Justice, on behalf of an individual, can pursue fines and penalties. The ADA also encourages the use of alternative dispute resolution (ADR) techniques such as settlement negotiations, conciliation, facilitation, mediation, fact-finding, mini-trials and arbitration to the extent they are appropriate and authorized by law. Individuals may recover attorneys' fees in appropriate cases.

E. SUMMARY

Individuals with attention deficit disorder and learning disabilities are considered individuals with disabilities and enjoy the right to be free from discrimination in the workplace under federal law when their conditions are of sufficient severity to interfere substantially with a major life activity such as working. To invoke the protection of federal statutes such as the Rehabilitation Act of 1973 and the Americans with Disabilities Act, the individual must establish that 1] he is an individual with a disability 2] he is otherwise qualified with or without a reasonable accommodation for the job, promotion, employment benefit or privilege which is being sought 3] he was denied it solely by reason of a disability and that 4] the RA or ADA applies to the case. On establishing the existence of discrimination, the individual will be entitled to reasonable accommodation. Reasonable accommodations are of three general types: 1] those required to ensure equal opportunity in the job application process 2] those which enable the individual with a disability to perform the essential features of a job and 3] those which enable individuals with disabilities to enjoy the same benefits and privileges as those available to individuals without disabilities.

10. RESOURCES

■ TEXTS

Gerber, Paul J. and Reiff, Henry B., LEARNING DISABILITIES IN ADULTHOOD (1994)

Greenhill, Laurence, Osman, Betty (editors), RITALIN, THEORY AND PATIENT MANAGEMENT, Mary Ann Leibert, Inc. (1991)

Hallowell, Edward M.,M.D., Ratey, John J., M.D., DRIVEN TO DISTRACTION, Pantheon Books (1994)

Kelly, Kate and Ramundo, Peggy, YOU MEAN I'M NOT LAZY, STUPID OR CRAZY?!, Tyrell & Jerem Press (1993)

Latham, Peter S., J.D. and Latham, Patricia H., J.D., ATTENTION DEFICIT DISORDER AND THE LAW, JKL Communications (1992)

Latham, Peter S., J.D. and Latham, Patricia H., J.D., LEARNING DISABILITIES AND THE LAW, JKL Communications (1993)

Smith, S.L., SUCCEEDING AGAINST THE ODDS: STRATEGIES AND INSIGHTS FROM THE LEARNING DISABLED, Jeremy P. Tarcher/ Perigee Books (1992)

Weiss, Gabriel, and Hechtman, Lily Trokenberg, HYPERACTIVE CHILDREN GROWN UP, The Guilford Press (1986)

Weiss, Lynn, ATTENTION DEFICIT DISORDER IN ADULTS, Taylor Publishing (1991)

Wender, Paul H. THE HYPERACTIVE CHILD, ADOLESCENT AND ADULT, Oxford University Press (1987)

■ AUTHORITATIVE SOURCES

ARMY REGULATION (AR) ¶ 40-501

This document sets forth the general criteria used by the Armed Forces in accepting or rejecting applicants and draftees. It is available through the Army and is not contained in the Code of Federal Regulations.

DIAGNOSTIC AND STATISTICAL MANUAL OF MENTAL DISORDERS (3rd. Ed. Rev.) (Cited as DSM-III-R);

DEA DOCKET NO. 86-52; 53 FED. REG. 50591 (1988) This document contains an excellent description of ADD.

LEARNING DISABILITIES: A REPORT TO THE U.S. CONGRESS, Interagency Committee on Learning Disabilities (1987)

LETTERS OF FINDINGS are authoritative rulings by the Office of Civil Rights (OCR), Department of Education, Washington, D.C. 20202 on the application of the IDEA, RA, and ADA as they apply to education. They are cited by Complaint Number, e.g. OCR No. 04-90-1617 (17 Sep 90) and are available under the Freedom of Information Act.

THE MERCK MANUAL

BOOKS AND ARTICLES

Brown, Dale S., STEPS TO INDEPENDENCE FOR PEOPLE WITH LEARNING DISABILITIES, 1980. (Institutional Support System of Pennsylvania, 150 South Progress Avenue, Harrisburg, PA 17109)

Grossman, Paul David, J.D. Employment Discrimination Law for the Learning Disabled Community. Learning Disability Quarterly of Fall 1992, Vol. 15, No. 4

Zametkin, A., Mordahl, T.E., Gross, M., King, A.C., Semple, W.E., Rumsey, J., Hamburger, S. & Cohen, R.M. (1990) Cerebral glucose metabolism in adults with hyperactivity of childhood onset. *New England Journal of Medicine*, 323(2), 1361-1366

■ NEWSLETTERS

ADDendum
Paul Jaffe, Editor
Box 296
Scarborough, N.Y. 10510
914-278-3022

The ADDVISOR
Attention Deficit Resource Center
1344 East Cobb Drive # 14
Marietta, GA 30068

ADDULT NEWS
2620 Ivy Place
Toledo, Ohio 43613

■ VIDEOS

ABC'S OF ADD, JKL Communications, P.O. Box 40157, Washington, D.C. 20016. (202) 223-5097

ADHD IN ADULTS, Russell Barkley, Ph.D., The Guilford Press (1993)

PICTURE OF SUCCESS, Featuring Pat Buckley Moss and Larry Silver, M.D. (Learning Disabilities Association, 4156 Library Road, Pittsburg, PA 15234. (412) 341-1515

■ ORGANIZATIONS

ATTENTION DEFICIT DISORDER ASSOCIATION (ADDA)
P.O. Box 972
Mentor, Ohio, 44061
(800) 487-2282

CH.A.D.D. (Children and Adults with Attention Deficit Disorder)
499 Northwest 70th Avenue, Suite 308
Plantation, Florida 33317
(305) 587-3700

COUNCIL FOR LEARNING DISABILITIES
P.O. Box 40303
Overland Park, KS 66204
(913) 492-8755

DEPARTMENT OF JUSTICE
ADA Information
(202) 514-0301

ELECTRONIC INDUSTRIES FOUNDATION
919 - 18th Street, N.W. # 900
Washington, D.C. 20006
(202) 955-5815

EQUAL OPPORTUNITY EMPLOYMENT COMMISSION
ADA Information
(800) 669-4000

HEATH RESOURCE CENTER
One Dupont Circle # 800
Washington, D.C. 20036
(202) 939-9320

JOB ACCOMMODATION NETWORK
(800) 526-7234

LEARNING DISABILITIES ASSOCIATION
4156 Library Road
Pittsburgh, PA 15234
(412) 341-1515

NATIONAL CENTER FOR LEARNING DISABILITIES
381 Park Avenue S. #1420
New York, N.Y. 10016
(202) 545-7510

NATIONAL CENTER FOR LAW AND LEARNING DISABILITIES (NCLLD)
P.O. Box 368
Cabin John, Maryland 20818
(301) 469-8308

PRESIDENT'S COMMITTEE ON
EMPLOYMENT OF PEOPLE WITH DISABILITIES
1331 F Street, N.W.
Washington, D.C. 20004
(202) 376-6200

NATIONAL CENTER FOR CHILDREN AND YOUTH WITH DISABILITIES (NICHCY)
P.O. BOX 1492
Washington, D.C. 20013
(202) 416-0300

NATIONAL NETWORK OF LEARNING DISABLED ADULTS
800 N. 82nd Street
Scottsdale, AZ 85257
(602) 941-5112

ORTON DYSLEXIA SOCIETY
8600 LaSalle Road # 382
Baltimore, MD 21286
(410) 296-0232
(800) 222-3123

Appendices

Appendix A

Sample Resume - Chronological

APPENDIX

Sample Resume-Chronological

JANE STERN

---

281 Pines Avenue
Woodbridge, Virginia 20902

Home Phone: (707) 555-1212
Leave Message: (202) 955-5843

WORK EXPERIENCE

Clerk-Typist

Alexandria Hospital, Alexandria, VA
Typed rough drafts into final product, reviewed correspondence for accuracy of spelling, punctuation, grammar, and format, received and distributed mail to office personnel, and maintained filing system. April 1992 - Present

Mail Clerk

IBM, Silver Spring, MD
Received and sorted company mail, maintained records of donations, and performed general clerical duties. April 1990 - August 1990

INTERNSHIPS

Clerical Assistant

Prince George's County Public Schools, Silver Spring, MD
Developed student recruitment packets for personnel office. Organized and categorized necessary information for the development of recruitment packets. September 1991 - November 1991

Vocational Trainee

Life Experience Activities Program, Silver Spring, MD
Successfully completed clerical training in collating, photocopying, filing, mail sorting, and other general office skills. October 1989 - June 1990

EDUCATION

Montgomery County Public Schools Adult Education Center
    Intensive Employment Training   September 1990 - March 1991

Life Experience Activities Program (LEAP)   October 1989 - June 1990

Paint Branch High School   September 1985 - June 1989

References Available Upon Request

Appendix B

Sample Resume - Functional

APPENDIX

Sample Resume-Functional

PETER KENNEDY
                                      1027 Ridale Road
                                      Potomac, Maryland 20904
                                      301-555-1212

JOB OBJECTIVE:

A position as a recreation program director.

SUMMARY OF QUALIFICATIONS:

- Extensive background in program design and implementation.
- Ability to work with multi-cultural groups and staff.
- Experience in coordinating a variety of activity programs for youth and adults.
- Knowledge of recreational activities and resources in the Metropolitan area.
- Ability to operate within a budget and supervise a staff of 50.

EDUCATION

B.A.   Rehabilitation, University of Pittsburg, 1980.
M.S.   Recreation Programming and Administration, University of Maryland 1982.

EXPERIENCE

- Organized, developed and implemented programs for Division of Community Recreation, Citizens with Disabilities. Programs included: adult education programs, movie theater, recreation newsletter, arts and crafts, youth activities and social events.

- Planned, scheduled and implemented travel programs for residents. Directed, planned and organized day trips, week-long trips and special trips.

- Scheduled and assigned tasks to staff of projectionists, recreation aides, and adult education staff. Trained, assisted, and guided enlisted staff. Recruited, trained, and assigned tasks to recreation center volunteers.

- Planned, scheduled, and implemented outdoor recreation programs that included white water rafting, hiking, and backpacking.

WORK HISTORY:

1988-1992	Camp Director, Chesapeake Camping Center for Special Youth, Annapolis, Maryland
1986-1988	Program Coordinator, University of Akron, Akron, Ohio
1984-1986	Asst. Director, PRC Camp Management, Inc., Frostburg, Maryland

AFFILIATION:

1983-Present   National Rehabilitation Association, Maryland Chapter
                             Program Chair, 1987-1989

REFERENCES: Available upon request

Appendix C

Sample Resume - Combination

APPENDIX

Sample Resume-Combination

Ali Jabar
1452 18th Street, S.E., Apt. T-8
Washington, D.C. 20859
202-555-1212

OBJECTIVE
Medical Technician

EXPERIENCE

✣ Supervised, scheduled, trained, and evaluated lab assistants.
✣ Collected and tested tissue samples using a variety of testing procedures.
✣ Conducted preliminary medical intakes.
✣ Maintain medical supplies for a 100-bed hospital.
✣ Coordinate data collection for studies involving up to 2,000 individuals.
✣ Familiar with dBase III, Lotus 1-2-3, and WordPerfect.

WORK HISTORY

Medical Technician   June 1990 - Present
D.C. General Hospital   Washington, D.C.

Responsible for all testing in a 200 bed hospital. Supervise staff of 30 lab assistants.
Responsible for hospital studies of AIDS and venereal diseases. Coordinate 2,000 medical interviews to collect raw data for study. Responsible for data input staff and preparing raw data for studies. Acted as the hospital liaison with local and national AIDS groups.

Laboratory Manager   March 1977- May 1985
Georgetown Hospital   Washington, D.C.

Managed staff, supplies, operations for hematology lab in 400-bed teaching hospital. Supervised three technicians, developed lab budgets, managed compliance with federal regulations and accreditation procedures. Promoted from previous position.

Laboratory Assistant   March 1977- May 1990
Georgetown Hospital   Washington, D.C.

Maintained medical supplies for 400-bed teaching hospital. Collected samples and conducted routine tests. Conducted preliminary medical intakes. Maintained medical files of all testing procedures.

EDUCATION

Bachelor of Science, Chemistry Major, Howard University 1977

VOLUNTEER ACTIVITIES

Homeless Shelter Volunteer

REFERENCES

Available Upon Request

Appendix D

Sample Cover Letter

APPENDIX

1404 Cowbridge Court
Virginia Beach, Virginia 23464

December 12, 1993

Ms. Joanne Torn
Human Resources Director
ABC Health Care Systems
6969 Broadway Avenue, Suite 450
Virginia Beach, VA 29384

Dear Ms. Torn:

I am writing in response to your ad in Sunday's edition of the <u>Virginia Pilot-Ledger</u> for an assistant administrator. With over 10 years of professional management experience and an M.A. in Healthcare Administration, I believe I can make a valuable contribution to the ABC managerial team.

During my 18 years' experience in the health field, I have successfully handled a variety of situations. My accomplishments include but are not limited to development and implementation of a budget; formulation of a means of evaluating employee performance; development of training programs; coordination of emergency room and medical clinic activities; and supervision of a staff of 100 people. The enclosed resume provides greater detail. I possess the capabilities one seeks in a manager: a capacity to make just and proper decisions under pressure: the ability to coordinate resources effectively in order to meet a common goal; the administrative know-how successfully to manage multiple projects at one time.

I would appreciate the opportunity to meet with you or your representative to discuss the potential fit between your position and my skills and experience. I look forward to hearing from you. Thank you for your time and consideration.

Sincerely,

Donald W. Cerphe

Enclosure

Appendix E

Sample Interview Questions

Questions Commonly Asked During the Interview

1. Why should I hire you?

2. Why do you think you might like this particular job?

3. Why would you like to work for this company?

4. What kind of person are you? Tell me about yourself.

5. What are your main strengths (skills, abilities, personality characteristics)?

6. What do you consider to be your main weaknesses? What are you doing to strengthen these areas?

7. Describe a time when you had problems getting along with a supervisor, teacher, or co-worker. What happened? How did you handle it?

8. What would you like to be doing five years from now?

9. Tell me about your last job and some things you liked and disliked?

10. How long would you stay with the company if this job were offered to you?

11. How do you work under pressure?

12. Please tell me about any work gaps in your employment history. What were you doing?

13. Can you perform all the tasks of the position with or without accommodation?

14. Have you ever been fired or asked to leave a job?

15. Have you ever been in trouble with the law?

2.

16. You don't seem to keep any job for very long. If we hired you, how long would you stay with us?

17. What are your salary expectations?

18. When would you be available to start work?

19. Would you be willing to work overtime and weekends?

20. What career goals have you set for yourself?

21. How do you plan to achieve your goals?

22. What do you really want to do in life?

23. What one accomplishment in life has given you the most satisfaction?

24. What have you learned from your mistakes?

25. In what ways will you make a contribution to our organization?

26. How would a friend describe you?

27. What are your preferred work habits? How do you like to get things done?

28. Why did you choose this occupation?

29. Where else would you like to work?

30. What motivates you the most?

31. What situations irritate you?

32. What is one significant problem you have overcome and how did you do it?

33. What is your chief ambition?

34. How much responsibility do you like?

35. Do you like to supervise or to be supervised?

36. Do you have any questions about the job?

Appendix F

Sample Thank You Letter

732 Healey Road
Silver Spring, Maryland 20865

January 17, 1994

Jill H. Smith
Human Resources Manager
XYZ Inc.
200 Circle Parkway
Columbia, Maryland 20981

Dear Ms. Smith:

Thank you for the opportunity to meet with you to discuss the file clerk position. I was impressed with the efficient, well organized filing system that you use.

During my interview, I did not mention that in addition to my three years of office experience, I have worked for the past year as a volunteer for Washington General Hospital, performing various office duties, including filing. I believe that my previous experience would enable me to fit smoothly into your Records Department and to contribute to the overall goals of the department.

Thanks again for your time and consideration. I look forward to hearing from you soon.

Sincerely,

Thomas Jones

DISCARDED

JUL 1 4 2025

ASHEVILLE-BUNCOMBE
TECHNICAL COMMUNITY COLLEGE

3 3312 00047 6770

HV 3005 .S942 1994

Succeeding in the workplac

Asheville-Buncombe
Technical Community College
Learning Resources Center
340 Victoria Rd.
Asheville, NC 28801